▼ Slow Down and Grow Something.

The Urban Grower's Recipe for the Good Life. Cultivate. Cook. Share.

Byron Smith with Tess Robinson

MURDOCH BOOKS

SYDNEY · LONDON

Contents.

94
Part Two: Seasonal plants and recipes

Introduction.

The garden is a place I've come to spend a huge part of my life. So much so, it's become my job to spend hours nurturing and harvesting plants, day in, day out. I love my job because people, places and plants all offer something new and exciting each and every day. Working with enthusiastic people to grow the food they love in new landscapes keeps the challenge fresh and the rewards fruitful.

For my partner Tess and me, the garden is our refuge and one of the calmest places in which we can be. It's a place for us to slow down from the crazy pace of modern life. In the garden, your mind can unwind, reflect and pause to appreciate the simple beauty of nature. As life becomes more hectic and the relentless pursuit to 'do it all' dominates our days, growing your own food is a rewarding antidote and a quiet escape from the stress of the modern world.

Living in Sydney for nearly ten years, we've found the need to create daily rituals that provide us with opportunities to slow down and cultivate our own recipe for the good life. We've discovered that gardening and cooking ensure we maintain a simple, meaningful life in the chaos of the city. Whether it's sipping a cup of tea as we water our herbs in the morning light, or spending 30 minutes a day tending to our vegie patch, gardening in particular provides us with a time for reflection and tranquillity.

Growing up on the South Coast of New South Wales, my brothers and I were exposed to the practicalities of growing food, maintaining an orchard and raising the odd calf, chicken or kangaroo. Providing food for the family, collecting rainwater and living resourcefully were all essential parts of growing up on an acreage – it's a lifestyle and upbringing I value dearly. The appreciation and principles I learned as a kid from the bush motivated me to re-create this lifestyle for the people around me in the city. I just felt that city living would be better for everyone if they improved their lifestyle and slowed down by focusing on the fun of gardening and creative cooking.

For those of you who already have a garden, you know that the size of the garden doesn't matter – it's the total experience that it brings you. Maybe it's growing the tastiest Meyer lemon you've ever had, or the satisfaction of knowing that your basil and chilli are within arm's reach when it comes time to flavour your favourite dish. The garden-to-plate experience can be as small or as big as you like – the important thing is to enjoy it. I think that the popular surf brand

'Soak up the outdoors, reconnect with your food, share with your community and live the good life.'

slogan 'Only a surfer knows the feeling' can relate to the garden-to-plate lifestyle, too. Only a gardener knows the feeling.

With its constant hum and everyday hustle, city life is quite the opposite of taking a moment to sit on a mossy log by a creek within a national park. This can sometimes mean that city dwellers feel disconnected from nature and long to be back in touch with the natural world. This connection is especially important for children growing up in the city who may miss regular opportunities to explore the great outdoors. I believe that easing off life's accelerator enough to allow you to truly connect to your creativity and grow your own food is a positive step towards

a more fulfilling life. While the hard work, juggle and stress of modern life continue to pull us in all directions until we are overwhelmed, the simple act of gardening forces us to be in the present moment. Our gardens help us to slow down, bring us back to earth and enable us to enjoy the simple things. I believe we need our gardens now more than ever.

I've had the genuine pleasure of gardening with people of all abilities, from kids at school through to the staff of large corporations. The common thread I've noticed is that we are all capable, caring growers when given the time and space to learn.

Tess and I wrote this book to not only tell the story of how we managed to bring the good life

from the farm into the city, but also in the hopes of teaching and inspiring people like you to do the same. It's easy to feel rushed, stressed and overwhelmed, and we often feel like the pace of modern life hijacks our sense of calm, but it's possible to add simple rituals to our daily lives to help us to slow down and smell the roses (or rosemary!).

We hope these garden tips and kitchen recipes inspire you to soak up the outdoors, reconnect with your food, share with your community and live the good life.

If you're keen to slow down and grow, then you're ready to go!

Let's get started.

Byron

Why Grow Your Own Food?

I live my life pretty well by the old adage that the journey is just as important as the destination. I've found that whether it's surfing, cooking or growing, this rings true throughout both my everyday life and my passions. While the modern-day mentality is to seek out the quick fix, or to purchase the end result, I'd hate to miss out on the joy and experience of immersing myself in the process and the lessons I learn along the way. For me, growing food is a labour of love, and I usually find the process more fulfilling than the final harvest itself.

Although many of us live busy urban lives, where space and time are often limited, we still yearn to enjoy our lives like our country counterparts. And really, why shouldn't we?

You'll see that this book is divided into two sections – Part One contains plenty of gardening advice, while Part Two explores the four seasons, including the plants you'll most likely be growing and harvesting during each season and the recipes we like to make using those seasonal crops.

Much of the world's food is grown in three very different climate zones – tropical, subtropical and temperate – so it's not surprising that planting and harvesting times vary from place to place. Your region might be too cool to grow mangoes, or too warm to grow apples, but we can all grow something, somewhere. Gardening will continue to surprise you with what's possible for as long as you dig it (pun intended!).

I think that rediscovering our passion for growing food will become a lot more important as the planet's population continues to increase, productive farm land is further fragmented and our tastebuds cease to find the tasteless, snap-frozen supermarket vegies all that desirable. You just need to see the queue at the supermarket after it's been closed for a public holiday to realise that the majority of us are totally dependent on the convenience of buying our fruits and vegies.

Unfortunately, urban living often means we don't have enough space to grow all of our own food, but if you look around and talk to others who want to grow, a location and an opportunity will soon arise. Let's celebrate this ancient skill. After all, it was the desire to grow food that allowed humans to transition from a nomadic existence into our current societies.

Besides, gardening is truly entertaining, addictive, rewarding and fulfilling, both physically and mentally – regardless of the likelihood of a world food shortage in the future. It also adds richness to your cooking by making the most of what's in season, and you can share your flavoursome bounty with friends, too! So get out there and make a start – there's a seed with your name on it.

Part One

Get into the garden

Garden Basics.

Some gardening books have titles such as *The Complete Book of Fruits, Vegetables and Herbs*, which, to me, feels like they are attempting the near-impossible task of providing a 'how to' for every single plant ever grown and eaten in the history of humankind. For the new gardener who simply wants to master the art of growing oregano or manage to keep a kaffir lime alive, we've narrowed it down a little. In this handbook, we've kept things simple and focused on 40 plants that we've grown ourselves in various urban landscapes, such as courtyards, backyards, rooftops, balconies, verges and green walls. We've chosen these plants because they've worked well for us and are the usual suspects on our dinner plates. For somebody starting their own urban garden who enjoys cooking with seasonal fresh produce, I think this collection of plants and recipes is the perfect starting point.

As this is an edible gardening handbook, it features recipes showcasing the plant you've just successfully harvested – bringing the produce to the plate without the need for a whole stack of other ingredients. You'll find snacks, jams, pickles, smoothies, cakes, cocktails and other sweet and savoury goodies to enjoy all year round. Relishing the fresh flavours of homegrown food is the best way to reward yourself for growing the produce you would normally buy anyway.

There are many different seeds, seedlings and established plants available at your local nursery or online suppliers. If you fancy a particular variety of radish, chilli or kale, then have a go at growing it. Maybe try two or more varieties so you can compare the growing success and taste the nuances between them. Try your hand at growing some of the wonderful old vegetables available – heirloom vegies have a unique story, appearance and flavour. One of my favourite ways to source seeds is to ask my neighbours for seeds saved from herbs and vegies that grew and fruited well in our local conditions.

We aren't chefs but we love our cooking, so we wanted to share our garden-to-plate accomplishments with you in the hope you'll enjoy some of the same satisfaction that we do. We created these recipes with sustainability in mind – there's a lot of preserving and stockpiling for months ahead, and using up what we have rather than heading to the shops for just a couple of items. We provide alternative herb or vegetable selections so the recipes are flexible and fun, even if you don't have all the ingredients.

For me, the art of cooking is like being on a wave – you're in the moment, making do with all the skills you have (or don't have!), because every meal and every wave is completely unique. Nothing's better than the gut feeling that it's all coming together in the kitchen – the ingredients are fresh and fusing well, the timing is right and the taste is more than you had imagined. It's about being smart and practical with what you've got and getting to know each plant along its entire journey from germination to consumption.

Climatic Zones
and Considerations.

With cities dotted around the world, it's not surprising that we grow a huge variety of plants in a range of climates. Farmers and home gardeners around the globe grow a mixture of native and exotic plants for many purposes – food, medicine, materials and pure gardening pleasure. They are highly attuned to the weather and, more broadly, the climate in which they grow their crops.

Most of the fruits, vegies and herbs grown in Australia originated from other parts of the world with similar climatic regions. Although native plants sustained Indigenous Australians long before European settlement, we generally prefer to grow exotic food plants. I've always been interested in growing a native substitute for an exotic where possible. This practice helps me connect to the land, giving me a better understanding and appreciation of the food and people that the land nourished before my time. For example, our native river mint (*Mentha australis*) has a distinct fragrance and refreshing taste, and it grows in the same conditions as exotic mint species.

▼

KNOW YOUR GROWING CONDITIONS

Your climate will determine what you can grow and at which time of the year to plant. Cities along the coast are sometimes prone to more climatic variables, with growing conditions often changing dramatically from one side of the city to the other. For instance, being closer to the mild air of the beach prevents frost, but frost remains a concern for those with gardens further inland. This difference in average temperatures and environmental conditions will certainly affect what can be grown and how ripe these fruits and vegies can become in a given season. For this reason, it's vital to observe which plants are doing the best in your local area when you're out and about.

When travelling, I like to visit the local botanic or community gardens to check out the edibles in season, comparing these to what I'm growing at home. If we look even closer, down to our neighbouring suburbs, we may find that different soil types, vegetation, water bodies and structures all create unique microclimates within our urban areas. You can take advantage of these microclimates to grow plants that would otherwise struggle in your area by enhancing ideal growing conditions. For example, a tropical microclimate often features full sun, protection from cold winds, radiated heat from solid structures (such as brick walls), watering of foliage and a rich soil. If you create a tropical microclimate in your garden, you might be able to grow and harvest some sweet bananas in a suburb with a subtropical climate.

WHEN DO I PLANT?

When planting seeds, we often ask: 'Is this the right time?'. However, if you're a seed that is about to be sown, you are actually more interested in the soil temperature than whether the autumn leaves are starting to fall. Air temperature can fluctuate daily, but the average soil temperature will be steadily rising or falling throughout the year. For gardeners trawling through the nursery or online seed catalogues, we can generally make a judgement based on our calendar. However, you can use a soil thermometer to show you when the temperature is just right.

One planting strategy that fails almost every time is relying on retail nurseries to only stock the current month's seedlings. I see people buying warm-season annuals, such as basil, tomato and eggplant (aubergine), in autumn – unfortunately, those seedlings will soon end up as compost. My advice is that, if you're heading to the nursery, you should take a list of the type and quantity of seedlings you want to grow for the current season, and not be tempted by what's on the shelves.

Depending on your local climate region, seeds and seedlings might have an ideal day, week or month to be planted. For example, if you miss the boat for a spring planting because you only managed to build your raised beds in the summer holidays, you can still prep the soil and plant other quick-turnover crops that will be ready to harvest before winter. Plus, your winter crops will be ready to plant soon.

The 40 plants I've chosen for this book are those I think you'll enjoy growing and using in your cooking. I've included basic planting times for each featured plant. However, I recommend that you also do your own research. Talk to an expert at a quality nursery or someone in the neighbourhood with a green thumb to discover priceless local knowledge.

Garden Layout for Small Spaces.

Planning the layout of your garden ... Oh, the hours you could spend pondering the options! I've been known to hang around in my own garden, contemplating the possibilities of what should go where, long after the kettle has boiled. When I check out new spaces for potential edible gardens, the first thing I consider is where the sun will be shining throughout the year – choosing a place with plenty of sunshine will ensure you get the most growth out of your plants.

I swear I've watched pumpkin tendrils climb fences before my very eyes on a hot summer's day. As a plant grows from a tiny seed into a full-blown vegetable, it uses the goodness of the soil – but it's also going to need as much sun as it can possibly get. From my experience, you need a space with at least six hours of sun per day to grow food. This is a good rule of thumb, at least until you start learning which plant needs more or less sun than its neighbour. For those with sun all day long, you're laughing – but for most of us, the urban landscape rarely provides us with such solar luxury.

YOUR HOME'S ASPECT

A garden that's clearly open to morning and midday sun is preferable. In the Southern Hemisphere, that's a north-east aspect; in the Northern Hemisphere, that's a south-east aspect. Often, my team and I need to get creative to find the sun-soaked spots around our clients' homes. We utilise rooftops and walls to take full advantage of those UV rays.

Your home's aspect is a crucial factor in creating a truly thriving and productive garden. In the Southern Hemisphere, we get excited about north-facing gardens as we can be assured of year-round sun, whereas the south side of the home may be completely shaded in the cooler months of the year (the opposite is true in the Northern Hemisphere). Winter is a time for ginger, cauliflower, cabbage and so many other great vegies, so we can't ruin our winter gardening opportunities by failing to create the perfect garden layout.

ENJOYING DECIDUOUS PLANTS

Learning where to place a deciduous tree or vine in the landscape can help you keep a balance of sun and shade throughout the year. Fruit trees such as fig, persimmon, pomegranate, apple and pear drop their leaves over winter for their dormant period. This leafless period also applies to deciduous vines, such as grape. In urban areas, tall deciduous trees do a great job of shading people in summer and letting the sun through in winter. Place your deciduous plants so they can not only provide you with fruits, but also pockets of sun and shade when and where you need them.

CLIMBING THE WALLS

Greening the walls around your home creates a cooler, calmer and more productive space. The simplest, low-maintenance, long-term way to green a wall is to place a climbing plant next to the wall and train it to grow up a fixed wire or similar. You could plant a perennial passionfruit directly into the soil, or some annual climbers, such as cucumber, in a planter box.

Another way to green a vertical space is to attach several pots to the area using steel reinforcement mesh and timber. You'll need someone who is handy with tools, as this custom-built option requires the mesh to be fixed securely onto the wall or fence. This design allows you to grow a colourful, multitextured wall of herbs, flowers and leafy greens that will make your cooking and dinner parties even more satisfying. You can hand-water the pots or, if you need the green wall to take care of itself, you can set up an irrigation system.

CLASSIC POTS AND PLANTER BOXES

Using a well-curated collection of pots is a simple and practical solution for growing plants on balconies or in courtyards. It also means that you can move the pots around to make the most of the sun throughout the year. There are many plastic self-watering pots on the market, all promising maximum yields. However, besides the fact that they don't work any more efficiently than the classic pot, I've yet to see one that looks appealing. Try grouping together three pots of various sizes in a sunny corner of your space.

A colourful combo – such as a fruit tree in the biggest pot, some leafy greens in the medium pot and mixed herbs in the smallest pot – always makes for a striking statement set-up. Staggering the height of your plants ensures they all enjoy some sun and also provides a layered look for the space. You can choose a mixture of different colours, foliage and flowers – it's your garden, so have some fun.

If you have a large, paved courtyard, a raised timber planter box with a built-in bench seat will provide you with more food, easy access and a place to stop and relax. The depth allows for plants to fill out to their optimum size rather than to be confined to a small pot. Soil temperature and moisture tend not to fluctuate when there's more soil mass. You can also plant a fruit tree in here to provide some shade on the bed if needed. Think of the garden omelette you could whip up every Saturday morning from a few square metres of fresh herbs and lush leafy greens. If you have a larger space and are keen to keep chooks, you can literally walk through the yard and grab a few eggs, your greens and a lemon – breakfast is served. The only thing you're missing is a pinch of salt!

GOOD IN THEORY …

When I started gardening, I was always astounded and overwhelmed when reading about the soil conditions required by each edible plant variety I wanted to have a crack at growing. Gardening books rattled off 100 different plants, which each needed individual soil conditions. Even the tables in these books confused me, let alone actually putting the theory into practice.

Imagine I've got about 2 square metres (22 square feet) of garden bed plus a few pots ready to go. I read the table in the book, and the first plant I want to grow apparently needs moist, well-drained, rich, slightly acidic soil. The next plant wants fertile, reasonably moist but still well-drained soil. The third plant requires moist, loose, friable, well-drained soil, while the fourth needs rich, humus-rich, light soil … and so it goes on.

Talk about fussy plants! At my house, I only offer a set menu. We don't have the luxuries of space or time for menu alterations, unfortunately. Similarly, if you're serving up dinner for the family, do you all enjoy the same wholesome meal or does each individual get slight variations of the same meal?

My solution? Just aim to build the best soil you possibly can and grow all your vegies together. How else can you possibly grow a fruit tree, some leafy greens and some herbs in the one bed on your balcony? From my experience of seeing the limited spaces we have to grow our food, particularly in an urban context, there are only two or three options at most, and the best one usually focuses on the plants' sun requirements rather than creating minor variations in the soil condition. If you're a commercial grower or have the luxury of owning several garden beds, then by all means start creating optimum soil textures, fertility and pH levels for different groups of plants to maximise your yields. But this book is for the urban grower who has to be resourceful and creative to maximise their yield in a smaller space.

WOULD YOU LIKE PHOTOSYNTHESIS WITH THAT?

As mentioned earlier, six hours of sun per day is the minimum for most edible plants. But if your garden doesn't get enough sun, don't despair – try mint varieties, turmeric, ginger, edible flower varieties, microgreens or mushrooms indoors. Other plants might survive in less light, but they will not be all that healthy or productive – they may fail to flower or fruit, or they won't bounce back after you have snipped some leaves for a salad.

Generally speaking, your garden will fall into one or more of these three zones:

- the shady zone, with unfortunately less than five hours of sun;
- the half-day sun zone, with a comfortable six to eight hours of sun;
- the full-day sun zone, which enjoys sun from morning to evening.

Look around your garden, and see what parts fall into each zone. I often use an app on my phone to show me where the sun will be in the sky at a given time of year. There are plenty of apps available that essentially do the same thing. Just log on, stand where you want your garden to be and point your phone in the general direction of the sun. You'll see on the screen the sun's arc through the sky over the course of a year. From this, you'll be able to count the hours of sun your garden will receive for any given day of the year. You might discover that your garden will receive around six to eight hours of sun over the warmer months but only two to three hours of sun in the middle of winter due to a building's overshadow. Or, who knows, maybe that huge London plane tree on the street will drop its leaves in winter and you'll have more light to grow your plants!

Your new-found urban-growing knowledge will soon have you pumping out the best produce around. You'll begin to notice where the sun shines, where the rain falls, how your soil works and, most importantly, what you enjoy growing, cooking and eating the most. So take this book and a beer into the garden, and ponder the possibilities.

Working the Soil.

We all grew up playing with soil and, as gardeners, we still do. As our appreciation and knowledge of soil improves, so does the quality of our homegrown produce and, consequently, our own health. Nutrient-rich and organically grown food is a reflection of the grower's passion and patience for creating and maintaining a biodiverse soil in which their plants thrive.

If you look at a soil map of any region, it has numerous soil types within different climatic zones, some of which grow crops to sustain us. Then consider our farmers, viticulturists, market gardeners and home growers, all working with various soil types, good and average, to grow the food we eat.

In coastal Sydney, where I help people grow food, we are always conditioning sandy soils due to the underlying sedimentary sandstone. Just a few hundred kilometres away, growers are blessed with richer soils due to ancient volcanic activity. These soils have a different colour, texture and structure to the sandy soils breaking my heart here in Sydney's east.

▼

GET TO KNOW YOUR SOIL

The good news is that you can dramatically improve your existing soil or even buy new soil prior to beginning your garden project. However, before you reach for your wallet, let's do a few backyard tests to see what you've got underfoot.

As a gardener, you'll need to focus on the first 30 centimetres (12 inches) or so of soil, as this is where most of the action occurs. Hopefully this top layer of soil has a good mix of organic matter that is home to invertebrates, such as worms, as well as other biological entities.

Start by digging a spade or hand trowel into the ground, and (without gloves) feel the soil with your hand, look at its colour and listen to the sound of it rubbing between your fingertips. You can even smell it if you like! Don't be worried if your neighbours see

you playing with your soil – they'll understand when you deliver your first harvest of juicy eggplants (aubergines) and prepare a bowl of the scrumptious smoky baba ghanoush from page 149.

Similar to the fresh sourdough you may have had for breakfast, the soil in your hand is made up of several key components. The five main components of soil are organic matter, water, air, minerals and living organisms. Whether it comes from a tropical rainforest, an arid desert or somewhere in between, each plant has evolved so that it can live in a soil containing a particular combination of these components.

SOIL TEXTURE

Soil texture is a physical property of the soil that is sitting in your hand. It refers to the size of the minerals and the proportions

of these particles in the soil – these are the sand, silt and clay particles. You can see and feel these particles as you rub a small amount of moist soil between your fingertips. Can you imagine how many large sand particles would dominate a handful of 'sandy soil' from a coastal backyard? You can see and hear the grittiness of the sand portion of the soil as you rub it between your fingertips.

On the contrary, if we took a sample from a volcanic region, we might find a loam soil higher in clay content and better for growing edible plants. Having finer silt and clay particles, this soil wouldn't feel sandy – it would be smoother and stickier, like a moist cake mix. We might classify this texture as a silty clay loam. Finally, if you've ever done pottery, swum in a dam or used clay as a face mask, you're already familiar with super-fine, smooth-to-touch clay and its extreme water-holding capacity. Soils with a high clay content are called a medium to heavy clay. In simple terms, soil textures can be generally classified as either sandy, clayey or loamy.

Why does soil texture matter? Because knowing your soil texture gives you clues to soil properties, such as how well it holds water, its general nutrient content and if it's going to break your back when you dig it. Here are the main properties of the three soil textures:

- **Sandy soils** – Drainage is a little too good, therefore water and nutrients tend to leach out faster.
- **Clayey soils** – Drainage can be poor, leading to poor aeration. The soil can hold on to nutrients.
- **Loamy soils** – As you would imagine, we need a happy medium between sandy and clayey soils to grow our food. A loam soil is the pick of the bunch! It has the ideal texture for growing plants, as it offers an ideal balance of the physical and chemical properties that are the backbone of a good garden soil.

SOIL STRUCTURE

Another physical property of the soil is its structure. The particles and organic matter in soil huddle together, forming unique arrangements of crumby aggregates. Air, water and plant roots need to pass through the soil, and they do so by making use of pore spaces between the aggregates. The pore spaces between any solid particles in the soil are known as macropores and micropores – they are the large and small gaps for water and air to pass through or be held for a period of time.

The sponge you use in the kitchen functions just like a good soil structure – it absorbs water well, but can drain to hold both air and water, remaining moist for some time. Organisms such as earthworms assist in maintaining good soil structure by moving through the soil, creating organic matter and nutrients as they go. Having a well-structured soil means less work for the gardener, as the plants have access to adequate water, nutrients and oxygen in the soil.

To improve soil structure, temperature and aeration, simply add some organic matter. As soil organisms break down this organic material, they turn a poorly structured soil into a moist, nutrient-rich soil. This mirrors natural ecosystems, which feature a cycle of nutrients passing between the living and the decomposing, with the odd natural disaster to shake things up.

Water and air

Plant roots take up water that is held in soil pores. In addition to getting a good drink, the plant obtains nutrients that have been dissolved in the water. If you want big juicy tomatoes, for example, then ensure your plants have access to plenty of water on hot summer's days.

Good soil aeration is key to giving your plant roots space to grow and work (transpire). Air passes through the micropores in soil, as well as voids created by soil organisms. You can help create space for air and water to penetrate by simply using a garden fork on compacted soil. You can also drive a long wire or screwdriver into a pot plant's soil to allow air and water to enter.

SOIL CONSISTENCY

If you're itching to dig up the soil in your backyard, verge or community garden and plant your first crops, then it is important to know your soil consistency. This refers to how well a soil holds together when it's cultivated. A soil will behave differently if it's worked when it's too wet or too dry, and cultivating the soil at the wrong time can make its structure worse. If the soil is dusty and blowing away in the breeze, add water and wait awhile; if you're making clods out of clay with your boots, then the soil is too wet and you need to come back next week. On that note, if you're working with muddy or sticky clay, try adding gypsum to improve the structure.

THE SOIL PROFILE

The soil profile encompasses the various layers of soil, from the topsoil in which your lawn grows through to the bottom bedrock. You may have seen a soil profile when a road is cut through a hill – there is a sequence of coloured soil horizons (layers) at various depths. Depending on where you live, you might dig through an organic layer followed by topsoil and then a subsoil layer in your garden.

If you're planting a full-sized fruit tree in your yard, it's a good idea to take note of the layers as you dig the hole. Can you see sand, loam, clay, rock, backfill or even building waste? Fill the hole with water, and test its drainage – your new fruit tree will detest having wet feet. Add a premium potting mix or soil to the hole and, if you have compost or manure, add this to the top only, where organic matter naturally occurs. Premium potting mix is actually an ideal soil structure in a bag, so you can use this to plant into – but feel free to add your preferred organic soil conditioners and mulch over the top for added nutrients and moisture retention. It's all about re-creating a natural soil profile when planting a tree (see pages 60–1 for more advice on planting a tree).

SOIL ORGANIC MATTER

The thin crust around our planet that supports plant growth and subsequently most life on Earth comprises organic matter and topsoil. Although we don't like to think about it too often, you and I – like all living organisms on Earth – will eventually end up back in the soil to continue the natural cycle of nutrients. But in the meantime, you can cycle other organic

Get into the garden

matter through your garden to keep it kicking along. In fact, adding about 10 centimetres (4 inches) of organic matter per year to your vegie garden should keep it bulked up. This can be in the form of compost, worm castings, manures, mulch, green-manure crops or your deceased goldfish. Adding organics increases the diversity of soil biology, including bacteria, fungi and invertebrates (soil microbes love a warm soil rich in organics!). These hungry organisms will typically eat about two-thirds of the organic matter in the first year, turning it into the plant nutrients, carbon dioxide and water that your plants need to thrive.

Humus (not the yummy Middle Eastern dip, hummus) is what remains after these soil organisms have been hard at work decomposing the range of organics you've added to your garden or compost. It works like eggs in a cake mix – it glues mineral particles into aggregates, which improves and maintains good soil structure for your plants. Not only that, but the more humus that is created, the better the soil's resistance to attack by pests and diseases. Humus also contains plant nutrients that are slowly released as it is broken down by the soil biology. It goes without saying that if you are a gardener, humus is your new best friend. So keep adding organic matter to your garden to maintain a strong soil 'immune system' with the added benefit of nutrients and ideal soil structure.

RECYCLING NUTRIENTS

Gardeners with compost recipes are aware that the materials they add to the compost influence the quality of the finished product.

The nutrient content of the waste you throw into your compost will be similar to the nutrient content of the finished compost. It's the same if you eat low-quality food – you can't expect your body to be rewarded with loads of vitamins and minerals and be feeling on top of the world. This is why gardeners are so particular about what gets thrown in the compost and what gets cast away. Experienced green thumbs may even add special 'goodies' – such as seaweed, charcoal, comfrey leaf, manure and rock dust – for extra nutrients. Compared to synthetic fertilisers, however, compost generally contains low levels of nitrogen, phosphorus, potassium and a number of other beneficial nutrients.

If your plant shows signs of a nutrient deficiency, you can apply a specific organic nutrient or even a synthetic fertiliser if you're desperate for a quick result. I don't think that synthetic fertilisers are a sustainable, long-term strategy for maintaining a healthy and biodiverse garden, but they're okay if you need to use them on the odd occasion. For instance, if a crop or fruit tree is struggling, you may need to act quickly with a specific, measured treatment before you lose the plant forever. Always do a pH test on your garden soil before adding a fertiliser, as correcting an acid or alkaline level will release nutrients locked up in the soil. This might sound complicated, but don't stress – there's more to come on pH levels on the following page.

Nutrients from organic matter

Of all the elements known to us, 16 are essential for a plant's life cycle:

- Macro elements from air and water – carbon, hydrogen, oxygen
- Macro elements from soil – nitrogen, potassium, phosphorus, calcium, magnesium, sulphur
- Micro elements from soil – iron, manganese, boron, copper, zinc, molybdenum, chlorine

The role that each of these elements plays in your garden is quite complex, but when the time is right it's worth doing some further research to get a basic understanding of them. This will help you to identify symptoms of nutrient deficiency as well as read fertiliser labels – and ensure that you have the best beets on the block. If you need to add more nutrients to your mix, look for an organic fertiliser that suits the plants you're growing.

SOIL PH

You've probably heard of things being acid or alkaline – lemon juice, water, blood, soil, toothpaste, milk and coffee – but what does that mean, and how does it relate to soil pH?
    Here are the key things to know about pH:

- Scientists decided that the concentration of hydrogen ions in things should be measured using a logarithmic scale from 0 to 14, where 0 is extremely acid, 7 is neutral and 14 is extremely alkaline.
- The pH level of things is compared to that of distilled water, which is neutral at 7.
- You can test the pH of your soil any time you want using a cheap, simple test kit from the nursery. It's as quick as brewing a cup of loose-leaf tea.

- The pH of soil can be either acid or alkaline, but the best range for most edible plants is around 6.5–7.
- At a pH of 6.5–7, all nutrients are available in the soil for the plant to absorb.
- If your soil is 5 or below, or 8.5 or above, certain nutrients are locked in the soil and the plants don't have the key.
- You need to amend the pH so that it returns to the optimum level required by your plants.
- If the soil is too acid, you can raise the pH by applying agricultural lime, dolomite or chicken manure.
- If the soil is too alkaline, you can lower the pH by adding cow manure, compost or powdered sulphur.

Above

During a pH test, closely observe the colour change after adding the indicator liquid and powder to the soil.

So remember to test your soil when you're starting a new garden, getting a soil delivery or simply doing a routine check-up every few months. Take a few samples around the garden so you can get an average.

SOIL CONTAMINATION

Unfortunately, urban backyards may have soil contaminants. For example, lead from paint and from the use of leaded fuel may have settled in our urban topsoil. Research from Macquarie University, Sydney, says that these contaminants are usually found in the top 5 centimetres (2 inches) of soil. You can have your soil tested by a lab before you cultivate your new patch. But, as a precaution, edible gardens are often grown in raised beds with a soil depth of around 40 centimetres (16 inches).

Despite claims of 'safe contaminant levels', there is the potential for specific plants to draw worrying levels of contaminants into their crops – so growing the plants in raised beds gives you peace of mind, as you know your food plants are growing in clean soil. As new research comes to light, it's wise to stay on top of the latest news on safe levels and the best ways to deal with particular contaminants.

Choosing a Mix.

All you want to do is waltz into the nursery, lug a few bags of soil onto your trolley and get back to business. But once you're there, the options overwhelm you. All of a sudden, you're paralysed by indecision. Soil, compost, potting mix ... and we haven't even started on the different brands yet! It's a mind-boggling choice when all you want to do is grow a few herbs.

To add to the complexity of your decision, the packaging of these products screams for your attention by claiming to have added goodies. And, of course, they all vary in price and quality quite remarkably. It pays to learn which products you need and why, as you'll probably require fewer items than you think.

So let's take the bewilderment out of your next trip to the nursery.

POTTING MIX

You're buying this because you have pots or small planter boxes, or you're aiming to plant some larger perennials (such as a lime tree or rosemary) in the garden and you'll need to backfill the hole.

You're looking for love. Some countries provide an indication of the quality of the potting mix on the packaging. In Australia, this comes in the form of a little red and white Australian Standard logo that indicates if the mix is regular or premium grade. Your local plant nursery should be able to guide you to the premium-quality option if your country doesn't have a grade or standard logo on the packaging. My advice to anyone, regardless of their budget, is to lash out the extra pennies and choose the premium grade. This potting mix will provide good air and water flow, retain nutrients and moisture and have a neutral pH. Most will also include slow-release fertilisers. Despite the goodies already inherent in premium potting mix, I usually boost it a little more by watering in some seaweed extract or worm juice and adding a dressing of compost on top to increase the level of beneficial microorganisms in the mix.

GARDEN SOIL OR TOPSOIL

You're buying this because you have poor soil quality, you are filling in low ground or voids in the yard, or you are substantially raising the height of a garden.

You're looking for quality. If you only require a few bags, stick to the same rule as potting mix and keep your eyes peeled for a premium-standard logo. However, if you need half a cubic metre (17½ cubic feet) or more, do your research and find a local landscape supply centre that delivers. Look for a soil that isn't too sandy, lumpy or full of sticks or other debris. Read the soil chapter (see pages 34–43) to get a better idea of what to look for in a soil. A pH level between 6 and 7 would be ideal, but is usually hard to find, so use a simple pH test kit to check your bulk soil on arrival. You may have to do some soil conditioning to bring it back in range.

PLANTER-BOX MIX

You're buying this because you've got some large planter boxes or raised garden beds (commonly made from either timber, brick or galvanised steel) to fill and require a big load.

You're looking for practicality. Essentially, you're after the same quality as potting mix but as a bulk buy. If you multiply the dimensions of your garden bed (L x W x H), you'll get the volume of mix required. You can usually order bulk mix by the half cubic metre (17½ cubic feet). Any excess mix can be added to your existing soil around the garden or even to your compost. If the same supplier also delivers bagged products, such as manure, compost, mulch or fertiliser, consider getting that delivered with the bulk mix to save you time. Depending on site access, sometimes smaller bags of mix are your best bet, but know that this will end up costing you more in the long run.

COMPOST

You're buying this because you haven't made your own yet! Making a good compost is like making a good stock for cooking – it improves structure, adds valuable nutrients and gives new life to an otherwise average soil.

You're looking for premium organic. As a general rule of thumb, I add 5–10 centimetres (2–4 inches) of compost to the surface of garden soil or planter-box mix and lightly blend it in. A good bagged compost may also contain manure, rock minerals, potash, zeolite, fishmeal, blood and bone, gypsum, seaweed extract, worm castings and more.

MANURE

You're buying this because your depleted garden soil needs organic matter. Composted manure can be mixed into the garden to improve the water-holding capacity of the soil, feed soil organisms, give plants the nutrients they need and bulk up the soil mass.

You're looking for bagged or fresh. In the city, it's unlikely you'll be throwing money into Farmer Joe's roadside honesty box in return for a bag of cow or pony patties. But if you do, compost the raw manure first to kill seeds, then dig it through your garden. Bagged manure from the nursery is likely to be composted chicken or cow manure. Chook manure is said to be 'hot' due to its high nitrogen and phosphorus content – it's higher in nutrients than 'cold' cow manure, which is low in nutrients but improves soil structure.

MULCH

You're buying this because it completes a garden's appearance, regulates soil moisture and temperature levels, prevents the soil baking in the sun (which would send the soil biology south), and hopefully suppresses weeds. Some mulches gradually decompose, providing the soil with nutrients and carbon.

You're looking for a soft touch. A suitable mulch for edible plants is sugarcane mulch or lucerne, spread over the garden to a depth of about 3 centimetres (1 inch). Apply a thinner layer in cooler months, so the sun can heat the soil a little – plants like warm feet, too. These light mulches are softer on the hands and knees in the garden. Woody mulches tend to cause nitrogen deficiency in edible gardens. Avoid using bark chips or any hard, heavy woody materials as mulch for this reason.

The Art of Watering.

Plants have naturally adapted to the climate in which they have evolved – that's why the plants in your local national park aren't expecting you to appear with a watering-can any time soon. The same goes for older, established gardens with shade trees, perennial shrubs and other hardy ground covers – they only need the occasional watering through summer or in times of drought.

On the other hand, your precious basil seedlings or freshly potted lemon verbena will need some extra TLC. A vegie patch requires more water than an ornamental garden, so choose a watering system that suits your garden size, your plant types and the time you can spend watering – this will help you get the best results. If you're working long hours or likely to go away frequently, an irrigation system will be your best friend. If you're around home a little more, a good hand-watering session every two or three days will be perfect – and you might just find it becomes your relaxation time.

Once you understand how water, soil and plants interact, you'll be growing some quality, juicy produce in no time – and I'm sure your indoor plants will benefit from your new-found knowledge, too.

WATERING METHODS

The first thing we need to do is to look at the various ways you can give your green friends a drink.

Watering-can

This method is useful for plants that are located where the hose can't reach. You can add concentrated liquid fertiliser, fish emulsion, seaweed extract or worm juice to the watering-can, to water in new seedlings or over foliage.

Hose

Buy the best hose you can afford, and attach it to the wall in whatever way suits your ability and space. Before using your hose, stretch it out and weigh down the two ends with some timber or bricks. Leave it like this for a day, and you shouldn't get any annoying kinks in your hose. Lastly, make sure you buy a quality trigger nozzle for the end – one with a jet and shower option is fine. Watering the garden is a time to relax, appreciate your plants and admire your hard work – so don't let a dodgy hose put a dampener on this experience.

Automatic irrigation

These systems take time and some initial cost to install, but they ensure that your garden receives a reliable amount of water at all times. A good system can effectively water your lawn, garden beds, pots, green roofs, planter boxes and any hard-to-reach places. Drip irrigation lines can be strategically placed under mulch so the water quickly enters the soil and reaches the roots directly, reducing evaporation. To be more waterwise, you can connect your irrigation system to a water tank.

Rainfall

Not surprisingly, this is the best form of water as it's natural and contains a small amount of nitrogen that plants love. Rainwater is drawn through the tiny holes (stomata) in plants' leaves, stimulating larger leaf growth. If you're growing leafy greens, try to combine any drip irrigation system with some overhead watering from the garden hose or watering-can at least once a week. It's always a good idea to take your indoor plants outside for an invigorating shower when it rains.

GOING DEEPER

As a self-confessed plant whisperer, I am acutely aware if a plant is thirsty or has sadly died from lack of water, but I realise that many novice gardeners are unable to tell the difference. Can you?

Following is an experiment you can try to see what a water-stressed or wilting plant really looks like. This will help you identify the symptoms, should they arise in the future. Plants obtain water through their roots and leaves, and lose it through their leaves via transpiration – which is part of the photosynthesis process. Like the carriages on a train, water molecules continuously tow each other from the soil to the top of the plant by cohesion. As a gardener, your responsibility is to make sure the train doesn't stop.

Here's your experiment (you've got to be cruel to be kind sometimes!):

1 Buy two of the same plant in small pots – ideally, try a tomato, chilli or basil. Place the pots in the location you plan to grow the plant, and water one plant but not the other.

2 Observe and compare how the leaves start to wilt when the plant transpires faster than it can absorb water. Tomatoes will temporarily wilt as a way of reducing the leaf face exposed to the sun, but they will bounce back during the night when the transpiration rate is less than the absorption rate.

3 If the plant cannot replace the transpired water at night from the soil, then it has reached permanent wilting point – it's basically flatlining.

4 It's okay if your plants wilt a little during a hot day, as this tough love encourages deeper root growth. But for better eating and good plant mass, you should generally keep your edibles well watered so they remain happy and unstressed.

NO EXCUSES!

There are many water-related excuses for the 'passive euthanasia' of plants.

– 'It wasn't my job to water/my friend forgot to water/I swear I watered them … '
Although watering needs to be a certain person's gig, to prevent underwatering AND overwatering, all people in your household should be conscious of the plants' needs. It's just like keeping your pet's bowl full of water.

– 'But I usually give it half a glass of water when I walk past it.'
A good soaking less often is better than just wetting the surface frequently. The roots of

the plant will grow stronger and penetrate deeper into the soil to follow the water rather than sitting just under the surface. Ensure that the water flows out from the holes in the base of the pot to maintain good soil moisture.

— 'The potting mix looked dry, so I watered it, but the water instantly flowed straight to the base of the pot.'

This is usually because the soil has become hydrophobic, meaning that the water pools on top and runs down between the pot sides and the soil rather than through the soil. If you notice this happening, repot the plant with new mix or add organic matter to the mix to improve soil structure. To stop it from happening in the first place, always use premium soil mixes and never let a soil dry out completely.

— 'When I hose the garden, I don't know if the soil underneath the mulch is actually getting any water.'

Check that your mulch isn't too thick. Hay should be 20–30 centimetres (8–12 inches) thick; sugarcane should be 2–3 centimetres (¾–1 inch) thick. Ruffle up the mulch with your hands if it seems a bit flat and water repellent. As you're watering, every few minutes or so perform an intermittent check by removing a patch of mulch to see if the soil is getting soaked underneath. How long you should water for depends on the season, soil type and plant type, including its stage of growth. A good rule of thumb is to water until you see pooling on top of the soil or until you can drive your finger into the soil and feel that it is moist to a depth of at least 10 centimetres (4 inches).

— 'I didn't realise the batteries for the automatic irrigation system had died.'

A common problem with irrigation systems is that you aren't as 'connected' to the garden as you think. Because you don't physically water them yourself, it's easy to forget about your plants. Remember, irrigation systems have their flaws, too, and they need to be maintained just like anything else. They're a good backup to have, as long as you're still spending time in the garden.

— 'All the plants get the same amount of water, but my lavender looks mouldy and sick.'

Know your individual plants' watering needs. Allow your plants to use the water in the soil before adding more, as this helps create a stronger plant with deeper roots. Smaller pots tend to dry out more quickly, whereas larger, deeper pots hold water for longer. If your plants are going to be exposed to sun all day long, go for bigger pots to allow for more water absorption. If plants are in morning sun only, shade or even kept indoors, they won't dry out as fast so can be in smaller pots. Keep your pots slightly raised on feet or plastic building packers/ shims to allow free draining of water – this is crucial to prevent waterlogging.

— 'But I had a self-watering pot.'

Self-watering pots were made so that we could be lazier gardeners. The reason your plants won't dry out is because they're wallowing in a pool of stagnant water. The downside to this is that they'll have less oxygen around the root zone, therefore stunting their growth. Saucers under pots should be there to catch water, not be used as water reservoirs.

Growing from Seeds and Seedlings.

When you're at the nursery or eagerly filling your online cart from the comfort of your lounge, it helps to have a list of the plants you want to grow for the coming season. This might include your top five favourite herbs, a few quick-growing salad greens and some long-term root vegetables. Regardless of what your heart desires, you will generally have a choice between buying the plants as seeds or seedlings. Knowing the differences between the two will vastly improve your growing success.

Seeds are far better value than seedlings, and you'll have a wider variety from which to choose. At the right time of year, some seeds can be planted directly into the garden and have a much greater success rate than seedlings of the same plant. These include plants such as coriander, carrots, beetroot and Asian greens. Some seedlings don't transplant well, as their fine root hairs get damaged or simply shocked during the move and never recover.

▼

WHICH SHOULD I BUY?

You can buy the seeds of particular plants and sow them into punnets to germinate. Once they grow to seedling size, you can transplant them into the garden. This allows you to raise seedlings in more favourable and protected conditions. Try growing edible members of Solanaceae (the nightshade family) – such as tomato, chilli and eggplant (aubergine) – in seed-raising mix indoors, then move them outside when the temperature is right. These guys are a little more forgiving than other plants when transplanted as seedlings, just make sure to water them in well!

You can also purchase seedlings from a nursery or garden centre and plant them straight into the garden as soon as you get home. This is fine if you buy plants that don't mind being handled and transplanted at seedling stage, such as various members of Brassicaceae (the cabbage family) – for example, kale, cauliflower, brussels sprouts and cabbage.

If a seed can be sown directly into the garden, this is the best way to go. I find growing from seed is the most efficient, economical and stress-free method for both you and the plants.

RAISING SEEDS

You can have frenzied online shopping sprees as a gardener – it's not all hard labour and frugality. I realised this when I discovered the colourful world of online seed catalogues! Like my fellow gardener friends, I always end up ordering an array of rare, heirloom, colourful and unique-tasting herbs and vegetables. The local nursery usually provides the tried and tested varieties, which are great but, trust me, it won't take long before you're hooked on germinating your own hand-picked seed varieties, too.

A seed contains the DNA of yesterday's plant generation, and the potential of that seed to provide food for us well into the future is priceless. So, how do we turn this morsel of plant energy into the food we eat? Here are some tips on raising the seeds from your latest shopping spree.

— Seeds are sensitive to temperature, light and moisture so, if you're not ready to plant them, store them in a cool, dark and dry place. Keep your seeds with your wine, and you should be fine.
— In terms of when to plant, the website or individual seed packet will tell you the best months to sow your seeds. But as marketing would have it, that sowing window can get a little generous when a perishable product needs to be sold. The sowing times are generally a good guide, but you'll learn to be more precise after trialling different plants throughout the year. Succession planting (see page 62) will help you understand how late in a season you can plant something before it runs out of time to grow or produce a crop.
— The edible plants we grow come from a range of different climates around the world. As our seasons change, the ambient soil temperature will rise and fall, too. In a natural setting, most seeds have made it into the ground and are waiting in the soil for their optimum germination temperature. As a grower with an exciting new packet of seeds in your hand, you have to know when your local conditions are right for those seeds to hit the soil and start growing.
— A planting calendar for your climate, words of wisdom from a local green thumb and some good old-fashioned trial and error will all help you get your planting times down to a fine art. A soil thermometer will also aid you in the decision-making process.
— A popular soil temperature range for most vegies is 20–25°C (68–77°F). Depending on your climate, your soil temperature is likely to pass through this range twice a year – rising through spring into the warm season, then falling again in autumn into the cool season. I tell my garden students that it's like swinging on a swing – we mostly plant when the temperature is going up or down but not when it's at the bottom or the top.
— We've found that coriander (cilantro) seeds are best planted well after the summer solstice, when the days are getting shorter. If we plant them around early autumn, they grow into robust, leafy plants during winter and finally flower and set seed in summer.
— Some larger seeds germinate more readily if you soak them in water the night before sowing them. This moistens the hard or corky coating, resulting in a quicker and more even germination rate.
— If the seeds are tiny, like grains of sand, it's likely they'll only need to be sprinkled

on the surface of the soil, where you can then give them a light misting with water. Fine seeds, such as those of lettuce, need sunlight to germinate, so only cover them with a light sprinkling of seed-raising mix or soil.

- Seed depth and spacing is a common question when getting your hands dirty for the first time. Aim to plant seeds at a depth that is double their size (for example, 5-millimetre [¼-inch] seeds should be 10 millimetres [½ inch] deep). The finer the seed, the more of them will fit into the row or pot. Little helping hands are better off with big bean or sunflower seeds, as they may be tempted to dump a whole packet of tiny seeds in the one hole! Plant more seeds than you need, and then thin out the seedlings.

- 'Thinning out' is your chance to follow Darwin's theory of natural selection ... leave the strongest seedlings, and gently pluck out the rest. This reduces competition and ensures individual plants are given the best opportunity to grow into strong, mature plants bearing the fruits of your labour.

SUCCESS WITH SEEDLINGS

Buying seedlings can allow you to bypass the time, skills and environmental conditions required to grow from seed. The time of year, your personal ability and the seedling variety might also affect your choice between seeds and seedlings.

- When you're choosing seedlings, less is always more. How many sweet basil plants do you really need? One healthy basil seedling has the potential to grow into a small shrub up to waist height and supply your kitchen from spring right through to autumn. But most people buy the fullest punnet crammed with over 50 seedlings! Unfortunately, they proceed to plant all the seedlings into a couple of holes and then let them all struggle. To give your plants the best chance at a healthy life, plant each individual seedling in its own spot in the garden, correctly spaced as per the punnet label. You will more than likely have many seedlings left over, so these can be given to your neighbours or dropped into the compost bin or worm farm.

- The best seedlings are the ones that have arrived fresh at the nursery that week. Buy the shortest, healthiest seedlings that will allow you to separate them without tearing any leaves and roots apart. If the punnet is hard to press in or roots are growing out of the punnet base, the seedlings are likely to be old and root-bound. Do not take these guys home with you.

- The seedlings you've bought may have been grown in a shadehouse and haven't yet been exposed to full sun, so avoid planting them on a hot, sunny day as the heat will stress them out. Water the seedlings before planting, and try to keep some of the potting mix around the delicate roots. Hold the seedling by a leaf rather than by the fragile stem, and plant it at the same height as it was in the pot.

- Water in your babies with some extra-diluted seaweed extract or worm juice

'If the little guys' leaves are wilting, it's been too long between drinks.'

from a watering-can. You really have to soak the soil to ensure you flush out all the air pockets. This ensures that the tiny root hairs can make contact with the soil water. Keep the soil moist by watering daily. As your babies begin to establish themselves over the next few weeks, start to wean them onto just a deep watering every two or three days. If the little guys' leaves are wilting, it's been too long between drinks.

- Give your seedlings a dose of seaweed extract, worm wee or other homemade plant tonic every one or two weeks to reduce transplant shock and add valuable nutrients to the soil. If you haven't already added a light mulch, such as lucerne or sugarcane, do it now because this will lock in the moisture and help maintain a stable soil temperature.

- About a month after planting your seedlings, you'll hopefully be left with more than enough survivors. Just select the biggest and best-looking seedlings, and pluck out the rest. It's better to have five big cauliflower plants with room for good sun and airflow than seven stunted plants all competing for space and light.

Now might be a good time to see what seeds are available online. You can join a club and browse online or just get a catalogue sent to you. Start making a wish list by selecting interesting varieties and plants that fascinate you. The more you are excited by your selection, the more interested you will be in their growth and survival and, hence, the more success you will have.

Planting a Tree.

The act of planting a tree deserves some serious thought, love and care. If you think about how long the tree could potentially live for and how much it can provide you over the course of its life, you'll realise that it deserves a proper transition from the pot it was raised in to its new home in the garden. Just like when you move house, you want a smooth, stress-free transition that allows you to depart your old home swiftly, with the least amount of fuss possible, and settle into your new place quickly and easily. Trees, and particularly their roots, need to be prepared properly before planting, which is an easy task if it is accomplished using two sets of hands.

Here's how to prepare your tree for the move and avoid any teething issues in its new home:

- Give the tree a good watering the day before planting to reduce stress on the day. Add some seaweed extract to the water if you have it handy.
- While it is still in its pot, place the tree in the preferred location in the yard. Ask yourself some important questions. How tall and wide will it grow? Will it get enough sun to flower and fruit here? Where will it cast its shade in years to come? Are there any utilities, solid rock or major tree roots down to 40 centimetres (16 inches) that could potentially get in its way?
- If you're confident with the chosen plant and its placement, dig a cylindrical hole that is a little deeper than the pot in which the tree is currently residing. A long-handled spade is the best tool for the job.
- This could be the moment you realise what a heavy clay soil is like to dig

through! If so, fill the hole with water. If it takes half a day to drain, you'll have to mound up the planting area with a better-draining soil mix.
- Place the tree on a small tarp next to the hole, and remove it from its pot. The tarp keeps things tidy and catches any potting mix you tease off the root ball. Cut off any circulating or pot-bound roots, then gently scrape and tease out the finer roots with a small hand fork or your bare hands.
- Place the tree in the hole, and use premium potting mix or garden soil to ensure that the tree is planted at the same level in the ground as it was in the pot. Don't place compost, manure or any organic matter in the bottom of the hole, as the decomposition of this material in the deep-root zone is actually detrimental to the tree. A sandy soil or premium potting mix with good drainage and aeration is the best substrate for around the root zone.

- Pack the soil around the root ball using gloved hands, and ensure there is a snug fit by removing air pockets. Then water the tree in well – imagine you're filling the pot it came in about five times over.
- Your organic matter, fertiliser and mulch can go on top where it naturally occurs, along with the organisms that will decompose the material into available nutrients. Be sure to keep the base mulched about 50 centimetres (20 inches) out from the trunk to avoid weed and grass competition with the tree roots.
- Lastly, it's time to consult with the weather gods – you want to ask that the next few weeks aren't too scorching hot and that you get at least a few days of good rain. Depending on what results, ensure that your tree gets a solid watering every few days for a fortnight, and, following that, just big weekly waters. If its leaves are wilting, that's a sure sign of a thirsty plant, so adjust your watering or irrigation frequency to suit.

Are you planting your tree into a large pot? Ensure that the pot's base has adequate holes for drainage. If not, get out the power tools and give the pot some more holes. The pot should always sit on feet or plastic packers to allow water to drain freely. Cover all the holes with a piece of flyscreen or shade cloth so your premium potting mix doesn't escape, and get your planting started.

Now that your tree is in its new home, enjoy all that it has to offer. Remember to help manage its growth by providing nutrients, controlling pests and pruning it when necessary.

Succession Planting.

If you plant 60 radish seeds this week, you'll have 60 ripe radishes on the kitchen table sometime the following month. Now that sounds like a successful horticultural production plan, especially if you have all your jars rinsed and ready for pickled radishes. If not, you may want to stagger your planting times to prevent a glut of vegies all ripening at once. This applies to many other quick-turnover crops, too.

While it's great to grow a wealth of produce all at once (five stars for enthusiasm!), it's important to use your time and space wisely. Plan ahead so you've got the right amount of each fruit and vegie popping up and filling your plate each month.

▼

IT'S ALL ABOUT PLANNING

When I taught a kitchen garden program at a local school, creative kitchen chef Mel and I would plan what the kids would grow and the meals they would create over the following school term. We also had to make sure that nothing ripened during the school holidays!

The idea is that you plant your slower-growing crops early in their season, so you know you're giving the plant the required number of days to grow, flower and ripen. Pumpkin (winter squash), cabbage, eggplant (aubergine) and tomato are some slower growers that will come through with the goods later in the season. Think of these slower growers as the main course at a restaurant, but you still want some nibbles and starters while you wait. Plant a succession of quick-turnover crops as well, so you've always got something on your plate. Some good choices include fennel, lettuce, peas, beans, cucumber, dill, shiso, rocket (arugula), beetroot (beet), bok choy and microgreens, to name just a few. Make sure you don't plant too many not-so-popular herbs or vegetables. If you don't usually eat it, it's probably not worth growing, especially if space is limited.

TO PLANT OR NOT TO PLANT?

If it's towards the end of summer or winter, you might have missed the opportunity to grow long-term crops, as the temperature and daylight hours are less desirable than earlier in the season. Read each seed packet to see if the 'time to harvest' will give your crop time to ripen before the end of the growing season. Don't get disheartened if you've come to the garden party a tad too late – there's always an improvement to make in the garden or some quick crops to grow. For example, if the label on the tomato seedlings says '120 days to harvest' and it's already cooling down, maybe choose some quick-turnover or fast-cropping varieties instead. Remember, the nurseries will still be selling seedlings that are 'out of time', so you need to know what to buy. Just have something growing in the garden at all times to keep the soil moist and the microbiology active and well fed.

I think it's worth being aware of succession planting to avoid wasting surplus food, but it also allows you to get the most out of your garden and feel rewarded for your work. It's okay to experiment with plants in your own garden's microclimate – you never know what you'll be able to grow until you have a dig.

Picking and Harvesting.

Gathering your ripe fruits and vegies is a triumphant moment, especially for long-awaited goodies such as your first-time bunch of juicy grapes or fat butternut pumpkin. But how do you harvest those fruits, vegies or leaves when you need them? It's generally best to cut each fruit or vegie from the stem using a sharp knife, scissors or secateurs. Try not to pluck a fruit or tear a vegetable off the stem with your hands, as this usually damages the plant. In addition, the produce you've picked will store better with some of the stem attached. Some plants, such as lemongrass and rhubarb, naturally break off quite easily when plucked, so you won't damage the plant in this instance.

▼

HERBS

These beauties are best picked and used fresh for fragrance and flavour – that's the benefit of having them on hand. If you need to store softer herbs, such as parsley, coriander (cilantro), dill, basil or mint, I find that wrapping them in a damp paper towel or cloth and placing them in the fridge keeps them sprightly. Bunches or sprigs of hardy perennial herbs, such as rosemary, thyme, bay leaf, oregano and sage, do well in a vase of water on the kitchen bench for easy picking. Fresh herbs contain aromatic oils, and their scent breezes through the home if they are left on display.

Dried herbs have their uses, too. I often have a big bunch of dried thyme in a wooden bowl in the kitchen for months. It is so handy to have strongly flavoured homegrown thyme at the ready.

Hardy perennial herbs grow thicker when they are used often. The continual cutting of the stem tips triggers more lateral leaf growth, so they naturally grow wider and bushier. It's also lovely to let herbs flower,

as the blooms attract beneficial insects and bees to the garden that help keep the balance. You can also use the flowers from rosemary, sage, thyme, English lavender, nasturtium, borage and bergamot in your recipes.

LEAFY GREENS

If you're harvesting leafy greens, such as kale, English spinach, silverbeet (Swiss chard), rocket (arugula) or mizuna, just cut the outer leaves off close to the main stem without cutting through or removing the inner leaves. For quick growers, such as cos (romaine) lettuce and bok choy, you should harvest the whole head at once by cutting off at ground level.

VEGETABLES AND FRUITS

Learn to know when each type of vegetable or fruit is ripe – check its colour and smell, see whether it feels soft to the touch and give it a taste test. Is it the right time in the season for the crop to ripen? If the plant has to come out early to make way for next season's soil prep, the crop might still ripen inside the house. You could even have a go at drying the crop for later use.

If you know that a big crop is on the way – congratulations! You will soon be able to provide yourself with wholesome homegrown food, and it's a skill you can use forever. Plan a recipe, and check if you need anything else so you're good to go. After we had picked our 300th jalapeño from our garden, we gave about 30 to our neighbour, Karen, and she returned with a jar of the best hot sauce we have ever tasted! Sharing a recipe or a big harvest always connects you with people and nature, just as food has always done in every culture.

OUR SUNDAY CO-OP

How long has it been since you created something with your hands? Or said to yourself, 'One day I'm going to make this'? Well, a bunch of our friends and us decided that we would get together for a homemade meal once a month so we could talk, eat and trade our latest handmade creations. You could make, grow or cook anything and bring it in bulk to swap for other goodies. I could take 12 jars of honey and bring home 12 uniquely made items, such as handmade candles, garden pots, condiments, ginger beer, kombucha, handmade oils, bath soaps/salts, seedlings or sourdough. We had so much fun doing the Sunday Co-op with our mates.

- We found that making one thing in bulk is far cheaper than buying or making 12 individual items.
- We enjoyed learning to make something new each month, then giving a little spiel about the process to our friends.
- It kept our creative brain firing, as we had something to work on over the month and

we anticipated what would be brought along next time (as your latest creation was kept secret until you presented it on the day).
- It got us back in touch with the art of sharing and trading.
- Everyone ate, learned and had fun, and we all walked away with a crate full of goodies – it's like having Christmas once a month.

If you have surplus food from your garden and recipes at your fingertips, you could initiate a Sunday Co-op with your friends. You never know what hidden talents are waiting to blossom.

Hens at Home.

We always had chickens when I was growing up. I still remember going down to the chook pen with mum at the age of six. When you live on an acreage, these outdoor enclosures can be as big as an urban backyard. Made from leftover red cedar from our home, the old henhouse was full of garden tools, tins of grain and a party of squawking hens.

The anticipation of how many eggs I might find always kept it exciting. Sometimes the local diamond python might be curled up with a few chicken eggs inside her belly. Or maybe a massive wedge-tailed eagle or sneaky fox had gotten inside and dined on one of our girls. Maybe the baby chicks had hatched out from under their broody mother. You just never knew what surprises awaited you down in the chook pen among the old gum trees.

▼

CARING FOR CHOOKS

Chickens are special pets to have when you're growing up, and they sure do teach kids about animal husbandry and the birds' role in the garden. I've enjoyed keeping chickens as an adult and have seen many families and even workplaces all sharing the responsibility of caring for these cute and quirky creatures.

Like any pet, you need to consider their welfare first. As they're social birds, you should keep at least three at any given time. Is the space you want to keep them in adequate? Do you have the time to keep them happy?

Chooks need a mixed diet of grains, layer pellets, greens, shell grit and small stones, and will happily accept most kitchen scraps. And don't forget about the fresh water! Our chooks had quite the penchant for porridge leftovers, although our kelpie, Rainey, was always sad to see the food go to them instead of her.

Chickens require an area with some sun as well as shade, plus plenty of fresh air. They like dust baths, a roost for sleeping as well as fresh ground to scratch and forage over. They also need regular health checks.

WHAT CHOOKS CAN DO FOR YOU

If you can create an ideal home for these feathered girls, then you'll all get along just fine. Around four or five chooks should keep a family supplied with plenty of eggs for eating plus manure for the garden. They can also scratch and work over old garden beds and clean up dropped fruits in the yard or orchard. But let them into your freshly planted and mulched garden bed, and the tears will be rolling down your cheeks in no time. You just have to stay one step ahead of the girls if they're on patrol around any precious garden beds, as they'll do their best to scratch up your freshly planted seedlings in front of your eyes.

You can find suitable breeds for various climates, so do some research and see what birds already live around your neighbourhood. You might be able to find somebody hatching some chicks, too. I always loved to care for chicks as a kid – and I still do, as an adult!

Life of Honey Bees.

Bees are a truly fascinating species and one that deserves much more respect than is generally given to them. Around 35 per cent of the world's food crops rely on pollinators such as bees to turn flowers into fruits and vegetables that we can eat. When you think about it, that's a huge responsibility for our buzzing friends. These guys get a lot of credit for their delicious honey, but often their job of pollinating plants is overlooked.

To say we would be in serious trouble without pollinators is a huge understatement. Imagine taking away 35 per cent of the food that is on our plates worldwide! That's a good enough reason for any of us to want to help keep bee populations strong and steady well into the future. I believe that bee conservation needs to start on a local level. Whether it's maintaining your own backyard beehive, growing bee-friendly plants or supporting local people who sell honey at the markets, we can all do our bit to help these guys thrive.

LEARNING ABOUT BEES

The history, biology and day-to-day life of bees are all fascinating topics, and there are many books dedicated to them. Let me tell you about my experience with bees, and hopefully it will entice you to do some further reading to get to know these little guys some more, or to even become a beekeeper yourself.

My first real experience with a swarm of bees was a memorable one to say the least. Back when I was studying horticulture at college, I received a phone call from the owner of the local restaurant where we grew produce and kept chooks and bees. He said, 'Mate, your bees are swarming!' My friend Grant and I dashed out of class and across the city to locate our swarm. We soon found them hanging from a lemon tree a couple of gardens away from our hive. It was a big, dripping basketball of buzzing orange bees. I'd never seen or heard anything like it before!

We hadn't actually caught a swarm of bees before, so we phoned a friend – Doug, the self-proclaimed 'beevangelist' – for some on-the-spot swarm-catching tips. With bee suits on, a trusty pruning saw in hand and a box at the ready, we removed the branch that was holding the ball of bees. With a good shake of the branch, the bees fell into the box and we closed the lid. We then transferred our buzzing friends to a brand new hive right next to the original hive in the garden. So, now we had two beehives, one headed up by Queen Beryl and the other by Queen Daphne. The experience for us was a thrilling one, but also one that inspired me to continue learning and sharing what I know about this spectacular species.

Bow to the queen

Before I knew much about bees, I thought that a swarm was the entire family of bees leaving their hive to find a new and improved home. But, in actual fact, a swarm of bees is a portion of the family moving out and finding a new home. A swarm is great news for the bee population. It means a particular hive is healthy and environmental factors have allowed a new queen to be born. Swarming is the bees' basic strategy for survival and for diversifying the gene pool. The new queen takes the throne in the existing hive, while her predecessor and friends swarm off to find a new tree hollow or similar camp, increasing the bee population.

In the case of my college-day hive, Queen Beryl laid her worker bee eggs in the hollow hexagonal cells of the hive, but the worker bees fed a special diet of royal jelly to one of the developing larvae, thereby hatching a queen instead of a worker bee. When Queen Daphne hatched, Beryl hit the road with some of her workers. And this is precisely how this superorganism moves around the land and keeps its species alive. So, if you see a swarm of bees, know that they are often at their most placid, as they are full of honey and not protecting a hive. Luckily, this makes catching a swarm of bees a relatively calm procedure rather than the frantic one most people would imagine.

HARVESTING YOUR HONEY

Hive maintenance and honey harvesting are similarly meditative activities requiring close observation and constant learning. What I love most about beekeeping is that when you open the lid to the hive, you can immediately see the female bees busily

Left
The entrance to this Langstroth-style hive is in the bottom brood box; two honey super boxes sit on top.

working away inside, some flying in with pollen and others on their way out to forage on flowers up to 8 kilometres (5 miles) away. You might witness baby bees chewing their way out of the brood cells to begin their 40-day life, or see the male drones with their big eyes or worker bees tending to the honeycomb and brood cells or doing other daily hive tasks. The hive is a busy place, full of activity. It fascinates me and everyone else who's experienced it alongside me.

Harvesting honey is the ultimate joy. Once you've inspected the health of the hive, and if there's enough honey for both the bees and yourself, you can get cracking on harvesting your share. We sometimes cut the honeycomb off the frames and keep it as is, or we spin the honey out of the comb so we have normal runny honey in jars.

If you have a healthy hive and the local nectar flow is adequate, you will have enough honey to keep you happy through all of winter. In a good season, you might get 50 kilograms (110 pounds) of honey. This liquid gold can become your bargaining power to encourage your neighbours to grow bee-friendly plants. Once they taste the sweet delicacy of fresh, local honey, they'll be happy to help.

LOOK AFTER YOUR FRIENDS

A few different hive styles are available, with the Langstroth hive being the most common. Whatever hive style you go for, your dedication to the bees and constant observation will naturally make you a good beekeeper.

If you're not quite ready to commit to a hive, you can still support the local bee population by planting a bee-friendly garden. Creating an organic, pesticide-free garden with year-round flowering plants will assist in keeping bee populations strong. You can buy 'bee-friendly' seed mixes at your local nursery containing a variety of flowering annuals and perennials for the garden. As an added bonus, the plants encourage a natural balance between beneficial insects and pests in your garden.

GO NATIVE

If you feel that European honey bees might be a little busy for you, have you thought about keeping a native or endemic bee species? In Australia, for example, the stingless bee species *Tetragonula carbonaria* is most commonly kept by people for pollination and conservation purposes and for the simple fun of watching them buzz around the home garden. These bees are as small as a grain of rice and fly at temperatures above 18°C (64.4°F) to forage up to 1 kilometre (⅔ mile) from their shoebox-sized hive. I've installed these hives at local schools and community gardens where the students and locals were fascinated by them and gained a new respect for bees.

A hive for native bees is a positive addition to any organic garden, but check that your area has diverse plant species to allow bees to forage successfully. You'll enjoy having native bees working by your side, pollinating your plants and keeping you company on those balmy days in the backyard.

Bees have mesmerised me ever since I caught that swarm and observed their social life over a few years. I have so much more to learn and appreciate from bees that honey isn't the motivation anymore. I'm just in awe of their way of life and want to help sustain a species that is vital to life on this planet.

Worms and Compost.

Puppies and other family pets are far more likely to be snuggled and photographed than a slimy worm, so why should you bother keeping a worm farm? Although less cuddly than their canine friends, worms are lovable in their own way. This love usually develops out of an appreciation for the benefits that the worms (and their by-products) provide to your garden. They help to improve and maintain well-structured, rich, organic soil, while reducing your home's environmental impact by turning kitchen scraps into nutrients that your plants just love to soak up.

▼ WORM FARMS

Whatever brand or shape you choose, a worm farm should allow you to feed kitchen scraps into the top box and remove worm castings and worm water from the bottom box. The look, size and brand are irrelevant if you've got this function down pat. Just make sure to keep your worm farm out of the sun and place it where the temperature is more consistent.

Your new worm friends will eat any leftover vegetables and fruits. Cut up larger pieces into bite-size chunks for your mates, as this will help them get through it faster. A worm's digestive system deodorises kitchen waste and turns it into bacteria-rich castings (humus), which are full of nutrients for your plants. As the castings accumulate, take a few handfuls to spread around new plantings. The neutralised castings have a pH of around 6–7, which is the ideal pH level to allow most plants and edible gardens to access existing soil nutrients.

You can also dilute the castings with water (one part castings to ten parts water) to create 'liquid gold'. This nutrient-rich liquid can be used on new soils, seedlings or any garden areas in need of soil conditioning.

Diverting kitchen waste from landfill and turning it into premium plant food and quality humus for your garden is a key organic-gardening practice. The truth is, you'll never be able to buy a product as good as this, and, to be honest, why would you even consider paying for it if you can make it easily at home? If you're taking the time to grow food, then why not indulge in the process of creating your own fertiliser from waste as part of your home's closed-loop system? What's more, I believe gardening and being exposed to good soil bacteria through the handling of humus as well as the harvesting and cooking of our homegrown organic food helps to increase the diversity of our own gut health, contributing to a stronger immune system.

Worm tunnels

Another method of gifting your kitchen waste to these hungry little troopers is to build worm tunnels out of PVC pipe and insert them vertically into garden beds and large pots. This is a great alternative to a worm farm if you are pressed for space. Take a 30-centimetre (12-inch) long pipe and drill numerous worm-sized holes into it, then add a tight-fitting lid. Insert your scraps through the hole in the top, close the lid and the scraps will go directly to the worms below. Put as many tunnels around the garden as you need. You'll be reducing your would-be landfill waste *and* improving the quality of your soil and plant health! It's a win-win situation.

COMPOSTING

The ability to create quality compost comes with practice. Once you have mastered the technique, you will find that your compost is your secret weapon for gardening success. There are many compost recipes online and in books. Every seasoned gardener has their own unique method and love for composting. So, what's the fuss all about?

Adding compost to your soil helps to create superb structure and increase microbial activity (the compost is food for beneficial invertebrates and bacteria). Just picture a forest floor, deep with leaf litter, good moisture and organisms of all sizes living and dying in a rich, biodiverse ecosystem. This constant natural cycle replenishes the soil and all the plants, animals, fungi and bacteria that thrive off it. Humans are also part of this cycle, so it makes sense for us to be involved in composting.

Now, let's bring this nutrient cycle to your backyard. You'll need to consolidate all your organic yard and kitchen waste, and process it in either a worm farm or compost. Before you get going, here are a few things to know about composting:

- Choose a compost system that suits your ability and garden size. Some require you to just lift a lid, while others involve harder work but offer fast results.
- Composting using a slow/cold system is when you gradually add waste to a common plastic compost bin and the waste breaks downs gradually. It's best to have two of these bins going at once, so you can keep the full one closed as the material is breaking down, while adding your ongoing waste to the other.

- Larger compost heaps with a volume greater than 1 cubic metre (35 cubic feet) heat up faster due to the heat given off by bacteria working hard to decompose the material. The pile needs to stay above 50°C (122°F) for a few days. After that, it requires turning every few days, then weekly, until it looks like rich soil from a forest floor.
- Tumbler-style bins are a little faster at composting, as you can easily spin them once a week to aerate the contents and keep the microbes comfortable. As an added bonus, they're vermin-proof and, as we've found out, kelpie-proof!
- Successful composting is about adding a good mix of materials while maintaining a carbon to nitrogen ratio of about 30:1. We don't want to bore you with a table of the typical carbon and nitrogen content of everyday organic matter, so simply start by thinking of 30:1 as a dry material to wet material ratio.
- Composting works well when the bulk of the contents are just a little moist – similar to a well-drained garden soil. Keep a straw bale, dry leaves or shredded paper handy. If the compost starts to look shiny, feel soggy or smell pungent, add some of the dry material. A mix suffering from these conditions is typically higher in nitrogen than carbon. Fruit and vegie waste, manures and green garden waste all contain more nitrogen than carbon, so they will therefore add more moisture to the mix.
- Composting is like baking a cake, but it's ready in months not minutes (and you probably aren't as excited to devour it with some ice-cream!). It will need time for the microorganisms to break down the materials. The length of time will vary, depending on the size and type of your compost system, as well as the materials inside. If you've got some space to spare, you can build your own compost piles out of timber sleepers and add all your waste at once.
- Your compost is ready when it has turned a consistent dark brown and none of the original waste material is recognisable.

Soon enough, upcycling waste into nutrients for the garden will become second nature. You'll get the hang of the process and find the method that fits best with your gardening style.

Balance and Biodiversity.

When we think of good garden health, we think balance and biodiversity. A natural ecosystem has its own way of maintaining balance through a rich biodiversity of plants, animals, fungi, bacteria and more. Plants naturally get their nutrients from the atmosphere, sun, water and decomposing organic matter in the soil. We, too, get our nutrients from a balanced diet ... and good wine, of course!

When we grow food, we like to see healthy, strong plants growing at a steady rate, free of pests and diseases. The plants we grow may be native or exotic, an old heirloom or new variety, organically grown or not. Either way, we have to provide the optimum conditions for them to thrive. To me, this means focusing on giving the plants the soil type they require and planting them in the best location in the landscape, preferably nestled with other beneficial plants – replicating their natural environment as much as possible.

▼

WHAT YOU CAN DO

Once established, an ornamental garden might be happy just being on its own and it may even outlive the gardener who planted it, without the need for a green thumb to tend to it. But our tasty little fruits and vegetables will need us to mother them a little more, supplement their diet when they're hungry and even step in when pesky critters such as the cabbage moth come to town. How much you choose to intervene when pests attack depends on your own garden philosophy. I believe that everything has its place in the garden. For example, aphids are lunch for ladybird larvae, which are dinner for the garden skink ... and so the food chain continues.

A soil suited to the crops you want to grow is the first thing to cultivate, as this forms a strong foundation for healthy plants. Once you're confident that the soil is ready, have some fun choosing a range of quality seeds, seedlings and plant stock from a reputable supplier. A wonderful way to encourage biodiversity is to have a garden boasting a variety of different plants and flowers throughout the year.

FEEDING YOUR PLANTS

Keeping your plants well fed and preventing nutrient deficiencies are also in our best interests as gardeners. Generally, our fast-growing food plants are heavy feeders, as most need to complete their life cycle in less than a year. Think of well-fed vegies such as pumpkins (winter squash), which can grow to extraordinary sizes. Choosing what to feed your plants will ultimately affect biodiversity in the garden. Organic

matter such as compost, manures, mulches, green manures, seaweed and other natural nutrient sources will offer your plants a slow and steady supply of food and will improve soils. It will also feed and sustain populations of fungi, bacteria and many hundreds of other plant-friendly soil organisms.

However, if you're adding organic matter to soil, you don't want to bring pests or diseases along with it. So ensure that it's composted to kill pathogens and weed seeds. Alternatively, buy it from a quality supplier who can guarantee that it's not full of toxins or unwanted waste material.

Occasionally, you will need to target specific crops with a macronutrient or micronutrient, such as potassium or iron, to boost plant health and subsequently deter the pathogens that can sense weak plants. When we're in need of iron we may feel lethargic, but plants lacking iron get chlorosis (yellowing of the leaves, with green veins). To improve our iron levels, we can take an iron supplement for a quick fix or modify our diet to bring our iron levels back up slowly. Similarly, we can feed our plants a measured amount of iron with a water-soluble fertiliser or add an organic source of iron to the soil or foliage.

Over time, you'll find your own set of gardening practices and principles that work best for you. With balance and biodiversity in mind, you'll be more conscious of the garden products you buy and the way you observe your garden each day. As a more sustainable, organic gardener, you'll be rewarded for your efforts with a strong, thriving garden producing nutrient-rich food for the home.

Tools for the Urban Grower.

If you think growing food might become a major interest in your life, then spend time and money on choosing quality tools for the job. This will make a big difference to your gardening.

My brothers are addicted to adventure sports. Over the years, I've watched them save their hard-earned money until they could afford the top-of-the-range gear and tools for pursuing their latest outdoor obsession. This gives them peace of mind that they can trust their gear in the field, have the correct tools to do repairs and enjoy the benefits of quality products that last. The old adage 'you get what you pay for' certainly applies to the gardening industry, too.

I recently saw a pair of secateurs retailing for under $7. The pair I use go for over $100. Quality cutting tools should be comfortable to hold, cut well, stay sharp, have replaceable parts and, with a bit of TLC, last for many years. I use a sharpening tool, sharpening stone and grease, plus a lubricant/protectant spray to keep them clean, rust-free and working like a dream.

As for the larger hand tools, such as forks and spades, you'll be applying a lot of leverage and force to these as you dig during the years to come. Think of how fit you'll be! The old mattocks, shovels and spades we used on the farm as kids growing up are still going strong. Keep an eye out for some of these old gems at garage sales or the local markets before lashing out on new tools. 'They don't make them like they used to' will be the likely reassurance offered by the sun-soaked veteran gardener as he hands you a digging fork that was forged before you were born.

WHAT DO I NEED?

Knowing what tools to buy comes down to the soil and plants you have as well as the type of jobs you'll do in an average year. We care for urban gardens across the city with a handful of trusty tools, and this is what we use:

- **A pair of scissors and a knife** – for cutting twine and other materials; for harvesting.
- **Secateurs** – for pruning vines, shrubs and trees; for harvesting. Secateurs will cut branches up to the thickness of your finger. To be honest, you can't really work in the garden without these guys!
- **Long-handled loppers** – the leverage and larger blade will allow you to cut larger, tougher wood.
- **Pruning saw** – for making clean cuts through larger branches up to the thickness of your wrist, but you could potentially cut larger pieces, depending on the type of wood. (Branches thicker than your wrist usually require a chainsaw. These machines are quite dangerous, so maybe stick to making your blood orange cake and call in an expert!)
- **Hand trowel and fork** – for planting seedlings, shrubs and trees; for garden

edging, weeding, repotting, loosening up soil around plants and mixing in fertilisers.

- **Short-handled hoe** – for creating rows in the soil, planting crops, digging out weeds and other repetitive soil work, as they are ergonomically better than the trowel for certain jobs.
- **Long-handled spade** – for tree planting, hole digging and general garden jobs. The long handle saves your back and gives you leverage. (Short-handled spades are good for smaller courtyard gardens or tighter work areas.)
- **Digging fork** – for aeration and mixing of garden soil and turning compost (although you can use a proper compost fork, which holds the material better).
- **Hard rake and soft rake** – use the hard rake for levelling soil and the soft rake for gathering together dead leaves and broken twigs for the compost.

OTHER EQUIPMENT

When teaching garden workshops, we often discuss what other materials or equipment one might need to start growing food. The gardening activities you might need to undertake include propagation, repotting, making soil mixes, creating natural garden remedies, harvesting, pruning, composting, worm farming and maintaining the garden.

To get you started, here's a list of the common items you'll need:

→ large plastic tub
→ bucket
→ watering-can
→ pump sprayer or small spray bottle
→ roll of jute/twine
→ bamboo stakes
→ gloves
→ plant labels
→ seed-raising pot or trays
→ pH kit
→ packers and mesh for pots and planters
→ small tarp
→ hose and hose nozzle
→ sharpening stone/tool

Our Food Philosophy.

To make a meal from the produce you've grown is one of life's simplest luxuries and greatest pleasures. We've never been more excited and curious about or connected to the taste of what we're eating than when we've sampled the delicacies we've grown ourselves.

There's something about the expectation, the surprise and the delight of harvesting, preparing and enjoying your own fresh produce. Every mouthful brings with it a story of triumph and contentment. I'll never forget the time my brothers and I helped Mum harvest our first corncobs – we roasted them in the oven, lathered them in butter and then crunched our little teeth into the bursting yellow morsels. The sheer delight of watching these juicy cobs grow from seed to the point where we were able to enjoy them with the family was something pretty special.

If you allow it, the garden can be your greatest teacher. It teaches you patience, perseverance and presence, and it rewards you for your hard work, mindful observation and loving care. The garden will teach you lessons for life and lessons for the kitchen. It will encourage you to experiment, get creative and learn to make things from scratch that, previously, you would have thrown in your supermarket trolley without a second thought as to its ingredients or origins.

▼

THE IMPORTANCE OF SEASONALITY

In a fast-spinning world that is constantly fighting to find new ways to feed its 7 billion mouths, we've lost touch with what real produce looks like and what is seasonally available to us. Whether we like it or not, both our successes and failures in the garden teach us lessons about the importance of seasonality and Mother Nature's way.

Growing our own food means that eating seasonally is not just an aspirational ideal – it's a daily way of life. We eat simply, healthily and mindfully, not because it's the trendy thing to do, but because it's so convenient when delicious and insanely fresh produce is located only a few steps away from our kitchen. Why would we bother eating anything else?

At our house, our weekly menu is a compilation of the best produce of the season. Our pantry is an assembly of the previous season's preserved goods. Our shelves resemble those of our predecessors, who really had no other choice but to eat seasonally. Back then, the only produce available at the market was what was in season. For example, you could only buy peaches in summer and broccoli in winter. Now, produce is available year-round.

Ripe and juicy peaches, for example, start to appear on our supermarket shelves in winter – and we should be asking why. Collectively, we have lost touch with seasonal growing and eating. Fewer and fewer people understand the patterns of the year and what this means for their plates, so this knowledge is not being passed on to the next generation. We now see a huge lack in awareness of not just seasonal eating, but also where our food comes from entirely!

With this comes an even greater problem for the modern world – food wastage. Growing our own food has made us far more aware of wastage and has meant that we've become both more resourceful and more mindful in the kitchen.

FEEL-GOOD FOOD

We've been lucky enough to have a prolific patch while living in our city home. This backyard bounty has included an abundance of fruits, herbs, vegies, eggs and honey. It's been a labour of love, with a sharp learning curve when it comes to succession planting. We've had to quickly adapt to harvesting, cooking and storing some rather large batches of produce. With a penchant for cooking and a disdain for wastage, we've developed many methods of 'using up'

what we've had on hand. The recipes in this book are a result of this way of life and thinking. We created these recipes to help us utilise all the produce we've managed to grow successfully.

We cook because we love to enjoy, share and trade food, and we have been lucky enough to live in wonderful communities of people who raise their hands to swap a bunch of fresh rhubarb for a jar of jam any day of the week. Having our own garden and taking care of others' gardens has proved to us that, no matter how small or how urban, a backyard patch brings people together to grow, eat, share and learn, keeping us connected to the earth, the seasons and our community.

Returning to a way of cooking, eating and sharing food which is similar to that of the people and cultures before our time has taught us that food grown with pride and cooked with love doesn't just fuel you – it sustains you long after the pesto has been licked from the bowl. We hope these recipes inspire you to make more things in your kitchen and encourage you to think about your food, where it comes from and, just as importantly, how it tastes.

So, here's to your future edible garden, full and happy bellies and blissful days. Happy harvesting!

Part Two

Seasonal plants and recipes

Spring

Plants: Coriander / Dill / Fennel / Lemon sorrel / Lemongrass / Chamomile / Fig / Edible flowers / Rhubarb / Radish

Recipes: Dill pickles / Coconut, ginger and lemongrass ice-cream / Strawberry chamomile smoothie / Fennel and pear slaw / Lemon sorrel and burrata salad / Fig and rosemary tart / Rhubarb and rose jam / Edible flower popsicles / Cinnamon roasted radish fries / Pickled radishes / Chilli, lime and lemongrass mojitos

When spring comes around, most of us are well and truly ready to wave goodbye to winter – I know this is particularly true for gardeners. The mornings are brighter, the days are getting longer and the air is fresh with new scents. The bees buzz from flower to flower as you eagerly plant your new seeds nearby. It's a time of excitement and anticipation, as you imagine what the coming season could hold for your patch and your plate. Tess and I love nothing more than springtime afternoons in the garden, beer in hand and kelpie at foot.

In our subtropical climate, we are about to plant all the seeds we ordered during winter. If you're in a cooler climate, you might have to wait until mid- to late spring just to be sure there is no chance of frosts or a final cold snap.

In spring, we plant our gardens with both slow- and fast-growing vegetables and herbs. The basic plan with the slow growers is that they have enough time to grow while the weather is warming through spring and summer. Tomatoes, pumpkin and eggplant, for example, can take four to five months to ripen, so we get them into the ground in early spring. In the meantime, we enjoy the company and satisfaction of some fast-growing herbs and vegies. If you have the space, you can keep planting these fast growers right through until autumn to ensure you have a constant supply. We plant out soft herbs – such as dill, coriander (cilantro) and basil – radishes, Asian greens, some leafy greens and edible flowers.

If you're planting in early spring, ensure that the sun is beaming into your garden and there is no overshadowing by buildings or trees. Some plants will be okay with half a day of sun, but it's always best to opt for the sunniest location possible. Think fast growth in sun rather than lagging growth in part-shade for the majority of edibles in your garden. And don't forget good soil, nutrition and regular watering!

Spring is the time to make things happen in the garden, so have fun and keep observing.

Spring Plants.

CORIANDER (CILANTRO)

Coriandrum sativum; Apiaceae
(carrot family)

Why grow it. A common annual herb, we always make room for coriander in our gardens. Both the leaves and seeds are used in many dishes and, as a bonus, the flowers attract beneficial insects and bees.

Where to grow it. Place it in pots close to your kitchen, along with your other herbs that require regular picking, or at the edge of your garden bed for easy access. Full sun will give you the quickest growth for soft herbs such as coriander, but half a day of sun will also be okay.

When to grow it. Always grow from seed, as seedlings dislike transplanting and are quite often damaged when groups of them are separated into single specimens. Coriander performs best when it is planted after the summer solstice. If you plan to use it weekly, a few plants should give you enough leaves. Succession planting of seeds every few weeks in spring will give you short-lived plants, but they are still worth having.

How to harvest. Cut the outside stems down low to the ground. Let at least one of your coriander plants go to flower for the pollinators, and you'll get seeds for replanting, too. The dry, brown seeds can be used for sowing or cooking.

DILL

Anethum graveolens; Apiaceae
(carrot family)

Why grow it. We use the fine leaves, seeds and flowers in cooking and to infuse our pickling recipes. Sharing the same family as fennel and coriander (cilantro), dill's umbrella-shaped flowers are another haven for bees and beneficial insects.

Where to grow it. Keep this annual in a bed or pot close to the kitchen but in a full-sun zone. We see it thrive in deep soil with regular watering.

When to grow it. Grow it in spring or autumn. Like coriander, it is best grown from seed.

From left to right

Coriander (cilantro),
dill and fennel.

How to harvest. Cut the outside stems down low near the base. Let dill flowers go to seed if you want to use the seeds in cooking or to replant later.

FENNEL

Foeniculum vulgare; Apiaceae
(carrot family)

Why grow it. Fennel has a sweet aniseed flavour, and you can use the swollen leaf bases, leaf tips, seeds and flower pollen. We often roast our fennel, or thinly slice raw fennel into salads or slaws. The delicate flower pollen can be used for its sweet flavour in desserts or teas. Like dill and coriander (cilantro), fennel is part of the carrot family,

so expect a similar flower structure and lots of good bugs and bees hanging around.

Where to grow it. Place it in the ground or in a raised bed in the sun, towards the back of the garden as it's quite a tall plant, growing to around 2 metres (6½ feet).

When to grow it. Grow it from seed during spring or autumn, as it tends to bolt to seed in hotter weather. If you have the space, plant seeds monthly in spring to get a succession of harvests.

How to harvest. Cut the leaf tips as required. The bases take around 15 weeks to develop if the seeds are planted in spring. Flowers/pollen and seeds will follow if the plants are left in the ground.

LEMON SORREL

Rumex acetosa; Polygonaceae
(knotweed family)

Why grow it. Lemon sorrel is a perennial that can be used to give salads a zing of tangy lemon at any time of the year, although I think fresh spring leaves have the best flavour.

Where to grow it. Lemon sorrel will do fine in sun to part-shade. One plant is enough for throwing a few leaves through a salad, so keep it in the front row of the garden where you or the kids can pick it easily.

When to grow it. Plant seeds directly into the garden during spring or summer. If you would like to have extra plants around

the garden or to give away, you can dig up and divide a clump of lemon sorrel in spring or autumn.

How to harvest. Snip leaves off at the base, and use them fresh.

LEMONGRASS

Cymbopogon citratus; Poaceae (grass family)

Why grow it. The leaves can be used to flavour drinks or brewed to make tea. The stalks are used in cooking. It's an easy-to-grow grassy perennial with long, strappy leaves that make it an attractive feature in the garden.

Where to grow it. Lemongrass will be fine in half a day's sun, but it loves the heat and can grow into a clump up to 1 metre (3 feet) wide. The serrated leaves can give seedlings and softer plants a hard time when it's windy, so, if necessary, keep it in a pot to stunt its growth.

When to grow it. The plant grows from seed easily in the warmer months. In spring, you can also split off a stem with roots attached (a stolon) from a bigger clump and plant that in the ground.

How to harvest. The fine leaves are sharp, so wear long sleeves and gloves. Grasp the base of a single stem, and pluck it out quickly for a clean break.

CHAMOMILE

Chamaemelum nobile; Asteraceae (daisy family)

Why grow it. The apple-scented foliage and the petite flowers are beneficial for insects in the garden. The flowers can be used to garnish desserts, add flavour to smoothies and make a soothing tea.

Where to grow it. The best place is at the edge of your garden or in a pot in full sun, so it can be the star of the show when it is in flower and you can watch the bees hang out.

When to grow it. Grow it from seed in spring or summer. Scatter the seeds, cover them with a sprinkle of soil and water gently. The seedlings will form a clumping ground cover throughout the warmer months.

How to harvest. Cutting back the flowers every few weeks will prolong the flowering period and allow you to harvest more over the summer months.

FIG

Ficus carica; Moraceae (mulberry family)

Why grow it. A lush fig tree is a common sight in older city suburbs, where gardeners once favoured edibles over ornamental trees. I'm sure you'll agree there is nothing quite like a fresh, juicy fig.

Where to grow it. Figs are medium-sized, deciduous trees that aren't too fussy when it comes to soil type. Prune the trees to keep them in shape. The fruits will grow on the current and previous season's growth. We recommend placing your fig in a large pot in a strategic sunny spot in the garden to create dappled shade in summer.

When to grow it. You can buy a healthy fig tree at any time of the year, but when a deciduous tree is dormant during winter, there's less chance of transplant stress.

How to harvest. Pluck the ripe fruits from the tree before the birds beat you to them, and simply enjoy eating them right there and then. You get bonus points if you can make your figs last the distance to the kitchen!

EDIBLE FLOWERS

Why grow it. Edible flowers can sometimes be the blooms of the vegetables and herbs we grow, or they can come from plants we specifically grow for the flowers. Thyme, fennel, rosemary, English lavender, chamomile, nasturtium, elderflower, chives, mustards, borage, bergamot and pineapple sage all have pretty, edible flowers that are great for garnishing salads, sweet dishes, cocktails or smoothies.

Where to grow it. Most plants with edible flowers need at least six hours of sun per day.

When to grow it. This varies between different species. Choose the flowers you want to grow, and then do some research on the best planting times in your local area so that you get the most out of them.

How to harvest. Flowers are delicate things and, once they are picked, they should be used that day. Ensure that you don't pick the flowers with your fingers. It's always best to use scissors so that you don't risk damaging the flowers.

RHUBARB
Rheum x *hybridum*; Polygonaceae (knotweed family)

Why grow it. Growing rhubarb is a sure-fire way to make you look like a great gardener. The big red stems and bold green leaves are easy to grow, and they look seriously impressive in the garden. With endless juicy stems to harvest, you'll always have rhubarb and rose jam to serve up!

Where to grow it. Plant crowns in your garden, and lightly cover them with soil. Allow the rhubarb plants to grow to a decent 1-metre (3-foot) size before harvesting them for the kitchen. You can also buy established plants in pots, then transplant these into a sunny spot in the garden.

When to grow it. Plant the crowns in winter, and allow them to develop for around a year before you start harvesting the rhubarb.

How to harvest. Pluck the stems from the base, and never take more than half the plant. The green leaves are poisonous, but they can be safely composted. Only use the red stems in your fresh and cooked dishes.

RADISH

Raphanus sativus; Brassicaceae (mustard family)

Why grow it. Radishes germinate quickly and can be ready in about six weeks. The smaller salad varieties come in a range of colours and sizes. This is the perfect vegie to pickle or to use fresh in salads for its peppery heat, lovely colour and great crispness.

Where to grow it. It is best to plant radishes in the garden bed in full sun to ensure a quick harvest of these little beauties.

When to grow it. You can grow radishes pretty much all year round. However, avoid growing them during the winter months in cooler climates. Experiment with different varieties over the year, and see which ones you like the most.

How to harvest. Pluck radishes when you can see them bulging just above the soil. This usually occurs between four and eight weeks after planting. Keep them well watered during the summer months to stop the bulbs from getting hard and pithy.

Dill pickles

In our house, it's hard to choose between a ploughman's 'picky' lunch and an actual proper meal. We almost always go with a ploughman's lunch. And what's a ploughman's lunch without some traditional dill pickles (aka bread and butter pickles)? These guys are the perfect balance of sharp and sweet. They remind us of lunches at the grandparents' place, where jars of their famous pickled cucumbers were served alongside crunchy crackers and tasty cheese.

Do

1 Combine the cucumbers and salt in a large bowl and cover with a tea towel (dish towel) for 1–2 hours.

2 Place the cucumbers into a strainer and rinse thoroughly under cold water. Drain well and place the cucumbers back into the bowl.

3 Toss the onion with the cucumbers and transfer the mixture to a sterilised jar.

4 Combine the remaining ingredients in a medium saucepan. Bring to a simmer over medium heat, stirring until the honey has dissolved. Pour the hot mixture over the cucumbers and onions in the jar.

5 Let the jar stand at room temperature for 1 hour. Place the lid on the jar and store the jar in the fridge for up to 3 weeks.

6 The pickles will be ready to eat after they have been in the fridge for 24 hours.

Use

6 small cucumbers, thinly sliced into rounds (generally the smaller the cucumber, the more flavoursome)

1½ tablespoons salt

1 white onion, thinly sliced

3 tablespoons honey

1 cup (250 ml/9 fl oz) purified water

½ cup (125 ml/4 fl oz) apple cider vinegar

1 teaspoon mustard seeds

1 teaspoon caraway seeds

2 dill flowers

¼ teaspoon ground turmeric

Oh and don't cut the cucumbers too thinly – you want them to have a little bit of crunch!

Coconut, ginger and lemongrass ice-cream

Serves 4–6

Anything with ginger and lemongrass gets our vote. This fragrant, refreshing and deliciously zesty dessert pairs well with Asian-inspired dishes. Although it falls within the dessert category, we've been known to indulge in this dish at all times of the day, especially during sweaty gardening sessions in the yard. This dessert is not one for the sweet tooths – it's decadently tangy and creamy, but not overly sugary.

Do

1 Peel off the dry outer layers of the lemongrass to expose the softer inner stalk. Cut off and discard the base and the dry top of the stalk, leaving only the soft portion. Roughly chop the soft lemongrass.

2 Whisk the coconut milk into the tapioca starch.

3 Place the coconut milk mixture, coconut cream, honey and coconut sugar into a saucepan over medium heat and bring to the boil.

4 Lower the heat and add the lemongrass, ginger and lime juice. Allow the mixture to simmer for 5 minutes.

5 Remove the saucepan from the heat and pour the mixture into a medium-sized bowl. Chill the mixture quickly by filling a large bowl halfway with ice cubes and placing the bowl with mixture inside, on top of the ice. Leave to chill completely, occasionally stirring the mixture. Alternatively, you can place the mixture into the freezer for at least 20 minutes, stirring occasionally.

6 Pour the mixture into an ice-cream maker and churn for 20 minutes. If you don't have an ice-cream maker, pour the chilled mixture into a food processor and blend for 1–2 minutes or until the lemongrass and ginger pieces have combined. Place the mixture into the freezer and leave it to set.

Use

2 lemongrass stalks

400 ml (14 fl oz) coconut milk

1 tablespoon tapioca starch

400 ml (14 fl oz) coconut cream

2 tablespoons honey

½ cup (110 g/3¾ oz) coconut sugar

1 fresh ginger knob (approx. 5 cm/ 2 in long, 3 cm/1¼ in wide), peeled and roughly chopped

Juice of 1 lime

Ice cubes

By the way, if you're feeling a little adventurous, try topping the ice-cream with a sprinkle of turmeric and chilli powder before serving.

Strawberry chamomile smoothie

Serves 4

As a young gardener, I was fascinated with picking and making mini-bouquets of chamomile flowers, but it wasn't until recently that I discovered the medicinal benefits of this beautiful herb. Chamomile is known for its calming effects, antibacterial properties and sweet aroma. The fresh or dried blossoms are most commonly used in herbal tea, but in the warmer months we like to sneak them into our smoothies.

Do

1 Steep the chamomile flowers in the hot water for about 5 minutes and then refrigerate until cool.

2 Place the cold chamomile tea (plus the steeped flowers, if you want a richer flavour) and the remaining ingredients into a blender and blend until smooth.

3 Pour the smoothie mixture into two glasses, garnish with the extra chamomile flowers and enjoy.

Use

2 tablespoons fresh chamomile flowers (don't use the stems or leaves), plus extra flowers for garnish

2 cups (500 ml/17 fl oz) hot water

4 cups (1 litre/35 fl oz) milk of your choice

1 cup (260 g/9¼ oz) Greek-style yoghurt

2 handfuls of ice cubes

1 cup (150 g/5½ oz) whole strawberries

2 teaspoons sesame seeds

1 tablespoon honey

Oh and if you have loads of chamomile plants in flower, you can create a big batch of this smoothie and freeze it in popsicle moulds for later.

Fennel and pear slaw *and* Lemon sorrel and burrata salad

Fennel and pear slaw

Serves 4 as a side dish

Fennel is one of our favourite vegies to both grow and eat. We once spent an entire trip around the coastline of New Zealand spotting wild fennel and jumping out of our van to devour the licorice-flavoured pollen. We manage to get fennel into many of our dishes, but this salad is one of the regular visitors to our weekly menu. Beautifully light and crunchy, it is the perfect side salad for a springtime barbecue, served up with barramundi or added to a hearty burger. The toasted almonds make for a great contrast in both texture and flavour.

Do

1 Place the honey, lemon juice, olive oil and wholegrain mustard into a glass jar. Seal the jar and shake it well to fully combine the ingredients.

2 In a frying pan over medium heat, lightly toast your slivered almonds until they are golden brown.

3 Toss the fennel slices, pear slices, slivered almonds, caraway seeds, salt and pepper in a bowl. Drizzle the honey mixture over the top. Garnish with fennel fronds and serve.

Use

2 teaspoons honey

Juice of 1 lemon

3 tablespoons olive oil

1 teaspoon wholegrain mustard

⅔ cup (90 g/3¼ oz) slivered almonds

4 fennel bulbs (remove the tough outer layer), thinly sliced

4 pears, thinly sliced

1 teaspoon caraway seeds

Salt and freshly ground black pepper, to taste

Fennel fronds, to serve

Feel free to add some finely shaved radish if you've got them popping up in the garden.

Lemon sorrel and burrata salad

Serves 4 as a side dish

Lemon sorrel is the underdog of the salad team. Its bitter greens have a subtle yet refreshing citrusy flavour and are prolific in spring. This particular salad is a favourite in our household for dinner parties and to pair with a Sunday night roast. With its slightly sweet, slightly tangy flavours, it also makes for a great topping on a freshly baked pizza.

Do

1 Preheat the oven to 180°C (350°F). Line a baking tray with baking paper.
2 Toss the tomatoes on the baking tray with the balsamic vinegar and olive oil. Add salt and pepper and toss to coat the tomatoes. Roast the tomatoes in the oven for 15 minutes and set them aside.
3 Place the lemon sorrel leaves into a salad bowl or on a serving plate.
4 Drain the liquid from the burrata, tear it into chunky pieces and add it to the lemon sorrel leaves. Nestle the warm tomatoes among the lemon sorrel leaves. Drizzle the juice released from the tomatoes over the salad.
5 Gently tear the mint leaves into smaller pieces and scatter them over the salad, along with the fennel seeds.
6 Season with more salt and pepper before serving.

Use

2 cups (300 g/10½ oz) cherry tomatoes, halved

2 teaspoons quality balsamic vinegar

1 tablespoon olive oil

Sea salt flakes and freshly ground black pepper, to taste

4 cups (120 g/4¼ oz) lemon sorrel leaves

2 large burrata balls, weighing 300 g (10½ oz) in total

2 mint sprigs

1¼ teaspoons fennel seeds

By the way, English spinach is often suggested as a substitute for sorrel. However, unless you add the juice of a full lemon to your dish, you will not get the tangy punch that sorrel has to offer. Sorrel has a citrusy flavour, whereas English spinach is more mild and earthy.

Fig and rosemary tart

Serves 10

Our family had a fig tree in the orchard at the property where I grew up. Us kids would sneak down there after school and gorge on the juicy morsels like hungry little fruit bats. Growing figs is not difficult, but making the figs last from the tree to the kitchen can be tricky! We avoided making tarts for a good part of our lives because the recipes seemed complicated and intimidating. So we've tried to make this recipe as simple as possible!

Do

1 Preheat the oven to 180°C (350°F). Lightly grease a 22-cm (8½-in) round cake tin with coconut oil or butter.

2 Combine the chickpea flour, almond meal, sugar, salt and rosemary in a bowl. Add the oil and rub it in with your fingertips until the mixture begins to stick together.

3 Spread the mixture evenly over the base of the cake tin. Bake for 12–15 minutes or until the base begins to change colour slightly. Remove the cake tin from the oven and allow it to cool completely.

4 For the baked figs, slice the figs in half and place them onto a baking tray. Drizzle with honey and bake for 15–20 minutes. You want the figs to start caramelising but still hold their shape. Remove the figs from the oven and set them aside.

5 Meanwhile, make the filling. Place the cream cheese, ricotta cheese, honey and lemon (juice and zest) into a food processor and blend until the mixture is creamy and smooth. Spoon the mixture onto the cold base and spread it evenly. Return the tart to the oven for 25–30 minutes or until the centre is custard-like. Remove the tart from the oven.

6 Top the tart with baked figs. Place the tart into the fridge for at least 2 hours before serving.

Use

To make the base

1½ cups (180 g/6 oz) chickpea flour (besan)

¾ cup (80 g/2¾ oz) almond meal

¾ cup (165 g/5¾ oz) coconut sugar (or raw [demerara] sugar)

Pinch of salt

1 heaped tablespoon finely chopped rosemary

2½ tablespoons melted coconut oil (or butter)

To make the baked figs

8–10 figs

Honey, to drizzle

To make the filling

250 g (9 oz) cream cheese

500 g (1 lb 2 oz) ricotta cheese

½ cup (175 g/6 oz) honey

Juice and zest of ½ lemon

Feel free to replace the figs with roasted pears in the cooler months.

Rhubarb and rose jam

Rhubarb and rose jam

Makes 4 cups (1 litre/35 fl oz)

The wonderfully sweet fragrance of this jam is enough to send you running for a slice of fresh, crusty sourdough. Our rhubarb seems to all shoot up at once. It grows like wildfire, erupting into pies, jams and compotes – enough for us and the neighbours twice over. Most traditional jams have a ratio of 1:1 between sugar and fruits, which to us is just far too sickly sweet. We prefer to use honey, but if you like traditional jams, opt to replace the honey with sugar.

Do

1 Preheat the oven to 180°C (350°F).
2 Place the honey and water into a small saucepan over medium heat and stir until the honey has dissolved.
3 Place the honey water, rhubarb, rose petals and salt into a bowl. Stir thoroughly so that all the rhubarb is coated with the liquid.
4 Transfer the mixture to a baking tray and bake for 1 hour, stirring gently every 20 minutes.
5 Remove the tray from the oven and set it aside to cool.
6 Place the cooled mixture back into the bowl and stir in the lemon juice.
7 Taste the jam for sweetness. If you desire more, stir in additional honey a few teaspoons at a time until you reach the desired sweetness.
8 Spoon the jam into sterilised jars and store the jars in the fridge for up to 3 weeks. Alternatively, place the jars into the freezer to make spring last forever.

Use

½ cup (175 g/6 oz) honey
¾ cup (185 ml/6 fl oz) water
1 kg (2 lb 4 oz) rhubarb stalks, cut into 5-cm (2-in) long pieces (discard poisonous leaves)
1 cup (40 g/1½ oz) fragrant rose petals
Pinch of salt
Juice of 2 lemons

By the way, any fragrant rose petals will do. All unsprayed roses are edible, with the flavour being more pronounced in the darker varieties.

Edible flower popsicles

If there's one ancient adage that we agree with, it's 'first we eat with our eyes'. This is why we garnish dishes with edible flowers from our garden. Effortless, easy and impressive, these floral popsicles are sure to entice both kids and adults alike with their bright colours and delicate taste. They're the perfect treat for a spring party in the garden.

Do

1 Half fill each popsicle mould with lemonade.
2 Place the flower petals inside the moulds gently, so that they don't stick together too much.
3 Add a couple of peach slices to each mould.
4 Gently top up the moulds with the remaining lemonade.
5 Insert popsicle sticks and place the moulds into the freezer for at least 4 hours or until the popsicles are frozen solid.
6 Remove the popsicles from the moulds and enjoy them in the sunshine.

Use

4 cups (1 litre/35 fl oz) lemonade (or coconut water)
Various edible flowers
3 peaches, thinly sliced

Feel free to swap the lemonade for Prosecco for a grown-up twist.

Cinnamon roasted radish fries

Serves 4 as a snack

This is always the first thing we make after our initial radish harvest for the season. These tasty little morsels are the perfect combination of crispness and sweetness, and they are a sure-fire way to curb any 3 pm sugar craving. As radishes are one of the fastest-growing vegies, they are a good one to get the kids to plant – they'll feel like green-thumbed superstars in no time.

Use

10–15 radishes, stem and root ends removed

1 tablespoon honey

1 tablespoon coconut oil

2 teaspoons ground cinnamon

2 teaspoons coconut sugar (or brown sugar)

Sea salt flakes, to taste

Do

1 Preheat the oven to 180°C (350°F). Lightly grease two baking trays with oil.
2 Thinly slice the radishes with a mandoline (be careful of your fingers!).
3 Stir the honey and oil in a saucepan over medium heat until they are perfectly combined.
4 Toss the sliced radishes in a large bowl with the honey and oil mixture and the cinnamon.
5 Lay the sliced radishes onto the baking tray. They can be touching but not overlapping. Sprinkle the radishes with coconut sugar and salt flakes. Bake for 30–40 minutes. You want to bake them long enough so that they lose most of their moisture, but they have not burned on the edges.
6 Remove the sliced radishes from the oven and set them aside to cool. They crisp up as they cool.

Feel free to add a dusting of paprika if you want a little kick of spice.

Pickled radishes

Makes 1 kg (2 lb 4 oz)

We first tried this recipe during spring when we had our very first home garden, and now it's a fridge staple. An easy side dish, it's tangy, refreshing, crunchy and the perfect palate-cleansing match for anything fried or slightly oily. Pickling is the perfect way to use up those extra radishes rearing their pretty little heads; you can store them and then add a little kick of vibrant ruby red to your meals all through the year.

Use

15–20 radishes, stem and root ends removed, sliced into thin rounds

3 garlic cloves

1 teaspoon mustard seeds

½ teaspoon ground black pepper

½ teaspoon seeds from a fresh chilli

1½ tablespoons salt

3 tablespoons honey

1 cup (250 ml/9 fl oz) white wine vinegar

½ cup (125 ml/4 fl oz) apple cider vinegar

Do

1 Place the radish rounds, garlic, mustard seeds, pepper and chilli seeds into a sterilised jar.
2 Combine the salt, honey and vinegars in a medium saucepan. Bring to a simmer over medium heat, stirring until the salt and honey have dissolved.
3 Pour the hot vinegar mixture over the radishes in the jar and let the mixture stand at room temperature for 1 hour. Place the lid on the jar and store the·jar in the fridge for up to 3 weeks.
4 The pickled radishes will be ready to eat after they have been in the fridge for 24 hours.

By the way, the heat from the chilli seeds in this recipe is not for the faint-hearted; if you dislike spicy dishes, feel free to leave out the chilli seeds.

Chilli, lime and lemongrass mojitos

We're not ones to turn down a cold, refreshing drink, particularly one made from fresh ingredients from our garden. Our twist on the classic mojito is spiced up with the heat of fresh chilli and the zing of lemongrass. The flavours are light and delicate, and they evoke lazy evenings sitting on the balcony and watching the waves roll in.

Do

1 First, make the lemongrass syrup. Bruise the lemongrass stalks using the back of a wooden spoon with some force.
2 Heat the water and honey in a small saucepan over medium heat, stirring until the honey has dissolved. Add the bruised lemongrass stalks and leave on medium heat for another 2–3 minutes. Remove the saucepan from the heat and set it aside to cool for 30–40 minutes. Discard the lemongrass.
3 To make the cocktail, place the lemongrass syrup, lime wedges, mint leaves and chilli slices into a bowl and mix together.
4 Place five ice cubes each into four cocktail glasses.
5 Evenly pour the lemongrass mixture and rum into each glass. Top with soda water and add a lemongrass stalk. Stir and sip.

Use

2 lemongrass stalks, chopped into 10-cm (4-in) pieces
1 cup (250 ml/9 fl oz) water
¼ cup (90 g/3¼ oz) honey
2 limes, each sliced into 4 wedges
1 handful mint leaves
2 fresh long red chillies (seeds removed), thinly sliced
20 ice cubes, to serve
320 ml (11 fl oz) white rum
Soda water (club soda), to serve
Lemongrass stalks, trimmed to use as stir sticks

Oh and if you've got them in the garden, feel free to add some Thai basil or kaffir lime leaves.

Summer

Plants: Lemon verbena / Mint / Chilli / Bean / Basil / Parsley / Cucumber / Eggplant / Tomato / Zucchini

Recipes: Lemon, zucchini and rosemary bread / Gin and cucumber popsicles / Tomato ketchup / Parsley salt / Lemon verbena and raspberry cordial / Chilli and orange oil / Garlic and parsley butter / Basil and strawberry kombucha / Smoky baba ghanoush / Garlic pickled green beans / Cucumber and ginger smoothie / Choc mint mousse

In our household, summer is a three-month-long celebration of life. The sky is bright, the sun is hot and the garden is alive. Long days at the beach roll into balmy nights spent in the garden with good friends and good food. We're busy harvesting honey from our beehive, picking our prolific cucumbers, tomatoes and basil, and regularly watering our plants.

If you spent springtime in the garden, hopefully by summer you're enjoying a full harvest of garden goodies. Maybe you've already traded a crate of colourful heirloom radishes? If you've just decided to get your garden in order now, that's great – check that you've got good sun for optimum growth. As you'll be planting winter crops in late summer/autumn, they will need plenty of light as the days get shorter and the sun gets lower in the sky. Check that your garden gets at least six hours of sun in winter by using an app or other source of local knowledge. You might need to raise pots higher, grow on a roof, rethink your plant choices or take over the footpath strip – whatever you need to do to chase the sun in winter.

Your herbs and edible flowers will probably be in bloom, attracting lots of beneficial insects including bees. A vegie garden mixed with herbs and flowers has the benefit of diversity, which will keep your plants happy. So continue to plant herbs and flowers, such as nasturtium, borage, perennial basil, echinacea, cosmos, agastache, salvia and heliotrope. It's easy to buy a packet of mixed flower seeds and simply sprinkle these into spare pots or other garden areas. In addition to helping the garden, you'll have an attractive flower supply for most of the year.

Summer Plants.

LEMON VERBENA

Aloysia citriodora; Verbenaceae (vervain family)

Why grow it. The lemon scent of the bright green leaves is like nothing else in the garden, and the leaves can be used to make herbal teas, flavoursome cocktails and even ice-cream. The tiny white blooms make lovely cut flowers. You can let it grow naturally or keep it shaped to fit in your garden. If you want to try to propagate lemon verbena yourself, the plants will grow from softwood cuttings taken in spring.

Where to grow it. A location in full sun is best, as this will bring out the oils in the leaves. It will grow up to 3 metres (10 feet) high in the right spot, for example in a sunny garden bed or a pot that's protected from the wind.

When to grow it. Find it at your local nursery in the herb section. It is often sold at seedling size and will grow quite quickly during the warm season.

How to harvest. Cut off a handful of stems as you need them, always keeping in mind the shape of the growing plant. You can also keep a bunch of these stems in a vase inside, so you can use the leaves for tea; the fragrance of the leaves will fill your home. You can crown lift the shrub to allow more room underneath to grow other plants, if space is limited in your garden. Just cut off all the growth from down low on the trunk and keep the top bushy.

MINT

Mentha species; Lamiaceae (mint family)

Why grow it. Mint species are perennial herbs that grow best during spring and summer. Common mint, peppermint, native mint and spearmint are some of the mint species that I like to have in the garden. Taste a leaf at the nursery to see if you like it first. You can also grow mint plants easily from a stem with roots attached (a stolon).

Where to grow it. Keep mint in a good-sized pot or planter box, and it will grow into a lovely fragrant

Lemon verbena.

specimen with easy-to-pick leaves. This will also keep it from spreading through the garden.

When to grow it. Grow mint in spring or summer from seed, seedlings or cuttings. They are herbaceous perennials, meaning they live more than a year but the above-ground leaves and stems die down in autumn or winter and reshoot in spring. Just cut back any dead or woody stems during winter.

How to harvest. Mint needs to have its leaves constantly cut back to keep the plant bushy and thick and to prevent it flowering and going to seed too quickly.

CHILLI

Capsicum species; Solanaceae (nightshade family)

Why grow it. You can grow a variety of different chillies – habanero, jalapeño, cayenne, bird's eye … the list goes on – and the heat/pungency rating of each is measured on the Scoville scale. The flavour changes as they ripen, so pick your chillies as they change colour and enjoy the heat. For me personally, the habanero is way too hot. We use cayenne for cooking, and the mild jalapeños I can eat straight off the plant. We harvested about 300 jalapeños from our last plant; the more you pick, the more they fruit.

Where to grow it. Pots are fine, but place them in full sun if possible. The size of chilli plants varies, but make room for a shrub up to 50 centimetres (20 inches) wide. You can grow chillies as annuals or perennials in warmer climates. The first year seems to be the most prolific for us.

When to grow it. Plant chillies in spring. Buy seeds and have a go at germinating some yourself indoors where it's warm, then transplant them once the weather warms up.

How to harvest. Cut off the fruits with scissors, and use them either fresh or dried. Keep harvesting to encourage new flowers and fruits.

BEAN

Phaseolus vulgaris; Fabaceae (legume family)

Why grow it. Summertime means beans. If you have space, you can grow bush bean varieties; if space is limited, however, you can grow climbing beans. A great thing about beans is that they are nitrogen fixers, which means they put nitrogen back into the soil.

Where to grow it. You need to provide a trellis or similar for your climbing bean tendrils to wrap around and clamber up. Full sun with good airflow around the vine is ideal. Plant your rows running north–south, so the sun can shine between the rows as it arcs across the sky. You can plant other taller-growing crops like this, too.

When to grow it. Grow beans from seed. Plant them in spring, when the soil temperature rises above 15°C (59°F).

How to harvest. The more you pick, the more they'll fruit! Constant picking of climbing beans will encourage more growth. Generally, bush beans will be ready almost all at once. Try succession planting if you have the space. You can use the young leaves and tendrils of climbing beans as a garnish.

BASIL

Ocimum basilicum; Lamiaceae (mint family)

Why grow it. Sweet basil is just one of the many varieties used in cooking. You could also try growing Thai basil, lemon basil or holy basil (tulsi). Most basil types have green or purple foliage and are best grown as an annual for their fresh, new leaves. The perennial basil you might have seen at the nursery is not really edible and is better grown as an ornamental bee-attracting plant.

Where to grow it. Basil is a tropical plant, so it loves the sun and heat. It does well in pots and garden beds alike. Plant a single seedling so it has room to grow into a compact bush up to 1 metre (3 feet) tall.

When to grow it. Plant in spring and summer, and keep cutting off the flower buds to encourage bushier growth. The flowers also reduce the taste of the leaves, so this is another good reason to reach for the scissors.

How to harvest. Snip off flower tips, cutting just above where the small stems or leaves protrude from the main stem. This promotes lateral growth, making for a bushier plant. Don't include the flower buds in your salads or cooking, as they are bitter.

PARSLEY

Petroselinum crispum; Apiaceae (carrot family)

Why grow it. I think this is the most common annual/biennial herb I see growing in home gardens. It is one of the most versatile ingredients, as it adds a fresh flavour to salads, sauces, pastas and more.

Where to grow it. Ideally, plant parsley in a spot with half-day sun to full sun. It will develop a large taproot in its second year of growth, so it will benefit from being grown in deep soil.

When to grow it. Spring and autumn are the prime times to grow it. Most novice gardeners have success with seedlings, but make sure you separate the seedlings carefully and plant them individually. Seeds tend to take three to six weeks to germinate in the right conditions.

How to harvest. Cut the outside stems from the rosette base. You can cut out the centre stem later if it's going to flower – this will give you a little more sideways leaf growth around the base.

CUCUMBER

Cucumis sativus; Cucurbitaceae (pumpkin family)

Why grow it. These beauties are easy to grow from seed in summer, once the soil reaches 20°C (68°F). You can expect to get around 15 fruits per vine if you're growing the Lebanese (short) variety. Try smaller types, such as 'Lemon' or 'Mini White', for pickling whole.

Where to grow it. They will happily sprawl along the ground, but training your cucumbers to climb up a trellis allows for good sun and airflow, while also freeing up the ground for other plants. Full sun is ideal, as shade and moist leaves can encourage powdery mildew. Cucumbers are best grown in the ground or a deep planter box.

When to grow it. Spring and summer are the prime times to grow it. Keep planting seeds while the soil is warm to maintain your supply of cucumbers.

How to harvest. You'll be busy plucking these guys off the vines, so if you have an abundance just eat them raw as you're working in the garden.

EGGPLANT (AUBERGINE)
Solanum melongena; Solanaceae (nightshade family)

Why grow it. The eggplant comes from the same family as the tomato, and it's a common crop to grow during spring and summer. Baked miso eggplant and smoky baba ghanoush (see page 149) are a couple of our favourite recipes featuring eggplants. Prepare to get a few kilograms of fruits off each plant if it's the popular 'Long Purple' variety!

Where to grow it. Grow the plant in the garden or in a deep pot in full sun. The branches will probably need to be staked to hold the weight of the fruits.

When to grow it. The plant will need four or five months to grow, flower and produce ripe fruits, so get it into the soil during spring for summer harvesting.

How to harvest. Eggplants feel slightly soft when they're ripe and ready to pluck from the bush.

TOMATO
Solanum lycopersicum; Solanaceae (nightshade family)

Why grow it. As a kid, I would play among rows of Mum's giant tomato plants. I distinctly remember the smell of the leaves, as well as seeing the red fruits ripening in the summer heat. However big your space, you can probably manage to grow either some cherry tomatoes in a pot, a short and bushy variety that will stand alone or, if you've got a bit more space, the larger varieties that grow more like a vine and will need staking. Unless you've found a good supplier of tomatoes at the local farmers' market, nothing compares to the taste and texture of homegrown, vine-ripened tomatoes. Try growing heirloom varieties for their various colours, wonderful textures and better flavour.

Where to grow it. Tomatoes love sunny open spaces, pots, planters and raised beds. Indeterminate varieties (which are usually the

Eggplants.

vine types that you need to train and stake) keep on producing fruits until winter, so you'll have an ongoing supply throughout most of the year. Determinate varieties (which are usually the shorter, bushier types) will have a big flush of fruits at the end of the season, and their size makes them better for smaller spaces. Avoid watering the leaves, as this encourages fungal problems – just one of the many diseases that can afflict tomatoes. You can buy books dedicated to the identification and management of pests and diseases if you feel like being more in control of the culprits.

When to grow it. If you want delicious-tasting, unique varieties, buy seeds online or see what heirloom tomatoes are for sale at your local markets or nursery. Plant them in spring and early summer. Tomatoes found in supermarkets are hybrids that have been bred for transportation and longevity – hard and tasteless fruits are usually the result of this sort of commercial plant breeding. Tomatoes aren't supposed to be as hard as apples!

How to harvest. Let the fruits ripen on the plant – they will usually fall off in your hand with a light twist. Tomatoes will also ripen once inside if for some reason you need to take them off the vine early (perhaps it's the end of season and they aren't getting any riper outside). Place them with some bananas or in a paper bag to speed up the ripening process.

ZUCCHINI (COURGETTE)

Cucurbita pepo; Cucurbitaceae (pumpkin family)

Why grow it. This is a super-quick grower – you'll be harvesting your zucchini just eight to twelve weeks after planting seeds. 'Black Beauty' is an easy-to-grow variety – just remember to give it plenty of room to ramble along the ground, as it will easily cover 1 square metre (11 square feet) of space.

Where to grow it. I find that allowing these plants to grow over the edge of a raised bed gives you space to grow other food in the bed while the zucchini ripen on the ground below. Any large expanse of sunny space is a good place to let your plants go wild. Remember, cucumbers climb but zucchini such as 'Black Beauty' are ground dwellers. Avoid wetting the leaves too much, as this can cause fungal growth. Make an organic spray to prevent fungal problems by mixing one part milk to ten parts water, and spray it over the leaves.

When to grow it. Starting in spring, plant seeds every six to eight weeks for a continual supply over the warm season.

How to harvest. Smaller zucchini are better for eating than the bigger ones. It's tempting to try to grow a record-breaker, but it might just end up in the compost.

Lemon, zucchini and rosemary bread

Makes 2 loaves

This one is for people who adore a savoury loaf. It's great toasted under the grill with some shaved cheese on top. Savoury, earthy and sweet, this is the perfect morning snack before work. We always bake two loaves at a time – one for us, and another for our neighbours. That way, we know we'll get treated to some of their kombucha when brewing time comes around!

Do

1   Preheat the oven to 180°C (350°F). Grease two 21 x 11 x 7 cm (8¼ x 4¼ x 2¾ in) loaf (bar) tins with coconut oil.
2   In a large bowl, combine the flour, baking powder, walnuts, rosemary and salt.
3   In a separate bowl, whisk the eggs. Stir in the zucchini, coconut oil, butter, lemon zest and honey.
4   Slowly add the dry ingredients to the wet, stirring as you go.
5   Divide the dough into the two loaf tins. Bake for 40–45 minutes or until the loaves are golden brown. You'll know each loaf is ready when you gently press down on the top and it bounces back.
6   Transfer the loaves to a wire rack and allow them to cool in the tin for a few minutes. Take the loaves out of the tins and place them on the rack to cool completely.
7   Serve slices with butter and ricotta, or toast them under the grill (broiler) with some cheese.
8   Freeze a loaf if you like or gift it to a neighbour.

Use

4 cups (600 g/1 lb 5 oz) spelt flour

1 teaspoon baking powder

1 cup (115 g/4 oz) walnuts, roughly chopped

2 tablespoons finely chopped rosemary

½ teaspoon salt

4 eggs

4 cups (540 g/1 lb 3 oz) grated zucchini (courgette)

¾ cup (185 ml/6 fl oz) melted coconut oil

½ cup (125 ml/4 fl oz) melted butter

1½ tablespoons grated lemon zest

1 tablespoon honey

Oh and if you've got more of a sweet tooth, replace the grated zucchini with the same amount of grated apple. Rosemary and apple is one of our all-time winning combinations!

Gin and cucumber popsicles

Makes 8 popsicles

What's a summer party without some ice-cold gin? Not a party in our books. Homegrown cucumbers have a taste like no other vegie, and combining them with gin on a hot summer's afternoon is a match made in heaven. These popsicles are so easy yet so fresh, and they will be the talking point of any party.

Do

1 Place the honey and water into a small saucepan over low heat. Stir until the honey has dissolved. Set aside to cool.
2 Thinly slice two of the cucumbers and add the slices evenly to the popsicle moulds.
3 Place the remaining cucumber into a food processor and blend until smooth. Using a sieve, strain the juice into a medium-sized bowl. Gently whisk in the gin, lime juice, tonic water and honey water. Divide the mixture among each popsicle mould, leaving a little space at the top to allow for expansion during the freezing process.
4 Freeze for 1–2 hours, then push popsicle sticks into place before returning the popsicles to the freezer for at least 3 hours or ideally overnight.
5 Serve on a hot summer's day!

Use

2 tablespoons honey
½ cup (125 ml/4 fl oz) water
3 cucumbers
½ cup (125 ml/4 fl oz) gin
Juice of 2 limes
2 cups (500 ml/17 fl oz) tonic water

By the way, if you want to do a G-rated version for the kiddies, replace the gin and tonic with 2½ cups (625 ml/21½ fl oz) of lemonade.

Tomato ketchup

Makes 4 cups (1 litre/35 fl oz)

Homemade tomato ketchup is so easy to make – there's no reason why you should buy the supermarket version. And, what's more, the flavour is incomparable! Stock up on tomatoes in summer when they are in season, so that you can enjoy this sauce all year round. This summer staple is perfect for slathering on hot fries or a breakfast burger. We slow cook our ingredients to bring out the sweetness of the homegrown tomatoes.

Use

1 kg (2 lb 4 oz) tomatoes, chopped into quarters

1 brown onion, finely chopped

2 garlic cloves, finely chopped

½ cup (125 ml/4 fl oz) apple cider vinegar

½ cup (175 g/6 oz) honey

2 tablespoons extra virgin olive oil

1 teaspoon wholegrain mustard

1 tablespoon sea salt

1 teaspoon cracked black pepper

Do

1 Throw all the ingredients into a slow cooker and stir to combine.
2 Secure the lid and cook the mixture for 6–8 hours (we put our slow cooker on before going to bed and let the mixture cook overnight).
3 Once it's done, allow the mixture to cool. Transfer it to a food processor and blend until smooth.
4 Place the sauce into a sterilised jar and keep the jar in the fridge for up to 3 weeks.

Feel free to add a handful of basil leaves to the mixture for extra flavour if you've got basil in the garden.

Parsley salt

Makes about 80 g (2¾ oz)

There are a few favourite ingredients in our kitchen that we can never do without. We reach for these without a second thought, and use them as religiously as liquid seaweed on the garden. Our batch-made parsley salt is one such ingredient. Sprinkle it on tomatoes for an easy summer salad; it's also a bold addition to any barbecued meat. And it's a great way to use up an abundance of herbs. If you're not a fan of parsley, you can replace it with basil, rosemary, thyme, oregano or coriander (cilantro).

Use

1 cup (20 g/¾ oz) whole parsley leaves

½ cup (65 g/2¼ oz) sea salt flakes

Do

1 Use a sharp knife to chop the parsley very finely.
2 Pour the salt over the parsley and continue to chop, until the salt is worked into the parsley and you have a unified mixture.
3 The salt will be slightly wet at this point. Spread the mixture evenly over a piece of baking paper and let it dry overnight. If you're in a hurry or live in a more humid climate, spread the mixture over baking paper on a baking tray and preheat your oven to 180°C (350°F). Pop the tray in and turn off the oven. Let the tray sit in the oven until the mixture is dry to the touch.
4 Store the dried salt in a sterilised jar. It will keep for 3–4 months.

Oh and this recipe is a great way to use up whatever herbs you have going crazy in the garden.

Lemon verbena and raspberry cordial

Makes 3 cups (750 ml/26 fl oz)

Working in the garden during the long, hot days of summer can be quite challenging. We often have a flask of this iced-tea cordial on hand for a sweet and refreshing boost when the sweat gets thick and the going gets tough. Raspberries pair well with lemon verbena, but they can be replaced with blueberries or strawberries if you like.

Use

3 cups (750 ml/26 fl oz) water
½ cup (175 g/6 oz) honey
20–30 lemon verbena leaves
10–15 mint leaves
Juice of 1 lemon
1 cup (125 g/4½ oz) whole fresh raspberries

Do

1   In a medium saucepan, bring the water and honey to the boil. Stir until the honey has dissolved. Remove the saucepan from the heat.
2   Add the lemon verbena, mint, lemon juice and raspberries. Mash the raspberries with the back of a fork. Cover the saucepan and steep for 15–20 minutes.
3   Strain the syrup through a fine-mesh strainer into a sterilised jar and set it aside to cool. Once cooled to room temperature, place the lid on the jar tightly and store the jar in the fridge for up to 2 weeks. Serve with ice-cold water.

By the way, use this method to make healthy cordials with any edible herb from the garden – it's easy!

Chilli and orange oil

Makes 400 ml (14 fl oz)

This dressing is so simple, yet so good. The orange in the oil counterbalances the kick of the chilli and makes for a slightly sweet dressing. We use it to brighten up a simple salad or pasta dish – you can even drizzle it over fresh avocado on toasted sourdough. Take advantage of the chillies while they are in season, and stock up for the cooler months.

Use

2 oranges
5 small, fresh, hot chillies
1½ cups (375 ml/13 fl oz) olive oil

Do

1   Using a vegetable peeler, carefully strip the zest from one orange. Try to keep each strip long, and avoid getting any of the bitter white pith underneath. Place the strips into a sterilised jar and set it aside.
2   Slice each chilli lengthways and remove the seeds if you prefer a milder chilli flavour. Add the chilli to the jar.
3   Zest your second orange and set it aside.
4   Heat the olive oil in a small saucepan over low heat until a few small bubbles start to form. Add the zest from the second orange. Let it steep for 30–40 minutes, ensuring that the oil doesn't burn.
5   Strain the oil into your jar, over the zest strips and chillies. Make sure your zest strips and chillies are fully submerged. If necessary, top up with a little more olive oil, as exposed fruits will turn mouldy.
6   Place the lid on the jar tightly and store the jar in the fridge. The oil is ready for use in 2–3 days. It will keep for about 2 months in an airtight jar.

Remember to keep a jar on hand for a last-minute gift!

Garlic and parsley butter

Makes ½ cup (125 g/4½ oz)

When you've got more parsley than you can handle, it's time to make parsley butter. Keep it in the fridge to slather on barbecued fish, piping hot corncobs or a slice of fresh sourdough. The best part about this recipe is that you don't have to use parsley – you can include whatever herb you have in abundance at the time! Because butter is always a good idea, right?!

Do

1 In a small bowl, combine all the ingredients. Mix well until the parsley is distributed evenly.
2 Spread a large piece of baking paper onto your kitchen bench. Place the butter mixture in the centre of the paper and shape it as best you can into a log.
3 Tightly wrap the log with the baking paper and secure the ends with twine or twist ties. Roll the wrapped log back and forth to create a compact, even shape.
4 Chill the butter in the fridge for 1–2 hours or until it is firm. It will keep in the fridge for 3 weeks, and in the freezer for 10–12 weeks.

Use

125 g (4½ oz) unsalted butter, softened to room temperature
¼ cup (15 g/½ oz) finely chopped parsley
2 garlic cloves, minced
1 teaspoon coarse sea salt
1 teaspoon freshly ground black pepper

Oh and depending on what you've got growing, you could replace the parsley with sage, thyme, oregano, rosemary or chives.

Basil and strawberry kombucha

Makes 12 cups (3 litres/105 fl oz)

Making kombucha is a regular ritual in our household. Like all fermented foods, kombucha is medicine for the digestive system and therefore the whole body. During summer, we almost always have a freshly bottled batch in the fridge ready to go. It's such a thirst quencher on those balmy beach days! Spend half an hour making kombucha every few weeks, and you've always got a brew ready to go. You can buy a scoby and starter tea from a health-food store; however, you may be able to find a friend or community member who can give you both the scoby and starter tea for free.

Do

1 In a large saucepan, bring the water to the boil. Add the sugar and stir until it has dissolved.
2 Remove the saucepan from the heat and add the tea leaves. Allow the tea to steep while the water cools to room temperature.
3 Place your scoby and starter tea into a sterilised jar.
4 Once the tea has cooled to room temperature, strain it into the jar.
5 Cover the top of the jar with gauze or muslin (cheesecloth) and secure with a rubber band (don't put the lid on the jar).
6 Put the jar in a dark place with good airflow (our kombucha loves sitting on top of our fridge). Leave it to sit for 10–14 days. Begin tasting the mixture at about day 10 – it should be mildly sweet and slightly vinegary.
7 Once you're happy with the final taste, use a large spoon and your freshly washed hands to remove the scoby. Place it into a sterilised jar with 200 ml (7 fl oz) of starter tea for your next batch.
8 Add the fresh basil and strawberries to the kombucha, pop the jar lid on and store the jar in the fridge. Once it is cool, your kombucha is ready to serve.

Use

8 cups (2 litres/70 fl oz) water
1½ cups (330 g/11½ oz) raw (demerara) sugar
2 heaped teaspoons loose-leaf black tea
1 scoby (kombucha culture)
200 ml (7 fl oz) starter tea
Handful of fresh basil leaves
⅔ cup (100 g/3½ oz) fresh strawberries, washed and hulled

Remember to have some fun experimenting with flavours from the garden – we also love pairing lemon and ginger, blueberry and sage or lime and raspberry.

Smoky baba ghanoush

Makes 2 cups (500 ml/17 fl oz)

Growing eggplants makes you look like a great gardener. They are so prolific – one minute there's nothing, and the next you've got enough to feed an army. The plant is lush and the fruits are abundant. This is a classic baba ghanoush we love for an afternoon snack or to lather on sandwiches. We prefer the texture slightly lumpy; if you like it silkier, feel free to use a food processor instead of the good old fork. We enjoy making ours on the barbecue, but you can also make it in the oven on high heat.

Do

1 Prick your eggplants on all sides a few times with a fork. Place them on the barbecue and cook them on medium–high heat for 35–40 minutes. The skin will darken a little and begin to smell smoky, but don't worry – this enhances the flavour of the dip. Set the eggplants aside and allow them to cool slightly.

2 In a medium-sized bowl, mix the tahini, lemon juice, garlic and salt.

3 Slice the eggplants in half lengthways. Drain the excess liquid. Scrape out the flesh with a spoon and add it to the tahini mixture.

4 Mash the eggplant flesh into the tahini mixture with a fork until it is smooth but with a bit of texture remaining. Allow the mixture to cool to room temperature and then stir in the parsley. Drizzle the dip with olive oil and garnish with the extra parsley leaves.

Use

2 medium eggplants (aubergines)
¼ cup (65 g/2¼ oz) tahini
¼ cup (60 ml/2 fl oz) lemon juice
3 garlic cloves, finely minced
½ teaspoon salt
2 tablespoons parsley leaves, finely chopped + extra leaves for garnish
1 tablespoon olive oil

By the way, this goes swimmingly with our rosemary and sea salt flatbreads on page 178.

Garlic pickled green beans

Makes 500 g (1 lb 2 oz)

We've found pickled green beans to be the ultimate companion to a decadent cheese platter. The refreshing and slightly crunchy texture beautifully complements the creaminess of the cheese. We always make a few jars of garlic pickled green beans at a time so that we can enjoy them through the cooler months, too. The best part about growing and eating beans is that the more you pick, the more they fruit!

Do

1 Place the beans, garlic, dill and fennel seeds into a sterilised jar.
2 Combine the salt, honey, water and vinegar in a medium saucepan. Bring to a simmer over medium heat, stirring until the honey has dissolved. Pour the hot mixture over the beans in the jar.
3 Let the jar stand at room temperature for 1 hour. Place the lid on the jar and store the jar in the fridge for up to 3 weeks.
4 The pickled beans will be ready to eat after they have been in the fridge for 24 hours.

Use

500 g (1 lb 2 oz) green beans
3 garlic cloves
4 dill sprigs
1 teaspoon fennel seeds
1½ tablespoons salt
¼ cup (90 g/3¼ oz) honey
1 cup (250 ml/9 fl oz) water
½ cup (125 ml/4 fl oz) apple cider
    vinegar

Oh and we often add cloves or replace the dill with fennel flowers for a more robust flavour.

Seasonal plants and recipes

Cucumber and ginger smoothie

Serves 2

Harvesting a cucumber is one of our greatest garden joys – once you try a freshly picked cucumber, the supermarket ones will never suffice again. The crunch and sweetness of a homegrown cucumber are delightful, but you can also turn these green wonders into a super-refreshing and tasty smoothie. Try this smoothie on a warm summer's morning, and you'll be hooked.

Do

1 Place all the ingredients into a blender and blend until smooth.
2 Pour the smoothie mixture into two glasses.

Use

1 large cucumber, sliced
1 heaped teaspoon grated
    fresh ginger
1 banana
¾ cup (185 ml/6 fl oz) fresh
    coconut water
Handful of ice cubes
Pinch of ground cinnamon

By the way, if you've got mint growing in your garden, add in some mint leaves for extra refreshment!

Choc mint mousse

This mousse is the perfect dessert for when you've forgotten to make dessert! A refreshing, healthy and easy twist on the classic crowd-pleaser, this dessert is so simple and yet so delicious. The mint washes away the sins of any feast, and it is one of the easiest herbs to grow. Every home garden should have some mint growing in it. It can thrive in a large pot if you only have a sunny little balcony or windowsill.

Do

1 Place all the ingredients into a food processor and blend until smooth.
2 Pour the mixture into serving glasses. Refrigerate for 1 hour before serving.

Use

4 large avocados, peeled, halved and stone removed
1 cup (20 g/¾ oz) mint leaves, finely chopped
⅔ cup (235 g/8½ oz) honey
1 cup (105 g/3¾ oz) cacao powder
½ cup (125 ml/4 fl oz) coconut cream
Pinch of sea salt

Oh and if you like crunch, add some cacao nibs to the top just before serving. We often replace the mint with half a teaspoon of finely chopped fresh chillies – chocolate and chilli were made for each other!

Autumn

Plants: Rosemary / Oregano / Pomegranate / Grape / Sage / Jalapeño / Carrot / Bees and honey / Lemon / Lime

Recipes: Fermented jalapeño hot sauce / Coriander, lime and garlic dressing / Rosemary and rocket pesto / Grape pizza / Pomegranate, apple cider and rosemary spritzer / Rosemary and sea salt flatbreads / Salted coriander and lime popcorn / Potato, sage and pecorino tarts / Pomegranate and salted dark chocolate bark / Oregano and gingernut cookies / Carrot and ginger Japanese dressing / Lemon curd with mint

By the time autumn rolls around, you've probably noticed the days getting shorter and the deciduous plants letting go of their colourful leaves, which fall onto the gradually cooling soil below. In the Southern Hemisphere, the sun reached its highest point in the sky during December (summer solstice); however, by autumn it's well on its way to brightening up somebody else's garden in the Northern Hemisphere.

The internet allows us to instantaneously view the gardening activities of our friends around the world. We can see the last beetroot being harvested in Brooklyn during autumn, while we wake in Brisbane to plant the same seeds for spring. We can observe all the seasons as they happen and appreciate the number of growing days we have in different climates.

In Sydney, the days are cooling down, but the ocean remains warm. Southerly swells are greeted with open arms, citrus fruits are ripening, while swapping and trading is in full swing as we make the most of the dwindling daylight hours and dusty pink sunsets.

In autumn, we may have already planted our winter vegies, such as broccoli or cauliflower, and may be putting in our peas and last succession of leafy greens. We might also be looking to get seeds into the ground so they can develop during the cooling temperatures and shortening days leading into winter. If you're starting your garden project in autumn, ensure that your plants will have enough time to grow before the winter chill sets in. Do they need four weeks, eight weeks or more to develop to a good size before the growth slows in winter?

Timing your plantings comes with practice. The more you talk to people and visit other gardens, the more you'll appreciate the unique climates we live in and the growing opportunities they offer.

Autumn Plants.

ROSEMARY

Rosmarinus officinalis; Lamiaceae (mint family)

Why grow it. A hardy perennial herb, rosemary grows up to 1.5 metres (5 feet) tall in drier Mediterranean climates. It's not a herb that needs a lot of water, but it does require full sun to thrive. Grow the main species for cooking, as many of the cultivars and the ground-cover forms aren't as good for culinary purposes.

Where to grow it. Rosemary likes well-drained soil and full sun.

When to grow it. It can be grown at any time of the year. Buy a good-sized plant in a 200-millimetre (8-inch) pot to get you started.

How to harvest. Cut the long stems at the base to encourage more long stems, or snip the top to make the plant bushier.

OREGANO

Origanum vulgare; Lamiaceae (mint family)

Why grow it. This hardy perennial herb is easy to grow in pots or as a ground cover in the garden.

Where to grow it. Oregano is happiest when situated in full sun. It will form an attractive mound in a pot or tumble over the edge of raised garden beds. Place it somewhere close to the kitchen, so you'll be able to access it for regular picking.

When to grow it. It's best to buy a little punnet or pot of seedlings, and plant them out in spring to late summer.

How to harvest. Use scissors to snip off the tips you need, as this keeps the plant bushy. A good cut back of the woody stems once a year in winter will ensure that the plant bounces back again in spring.

POMEGRANATE

Punica granatum; Lythraceae (loosestrife family)

Why grow it. A deciduous tree in cooler climates but evergreen where it's warmer, it has beautiful red flowers before fruiting. The

Oregano.

From left to right

Grapes, pomegranate and sage.

pomegranate is a versatile tree, which can be used in the landscape for its shade, foliage and fruit colour. It grows 6–8 metres (20–26 feet) in height and is super hardy and drought tolerant; it only needs a light pruning for shape.

Where to grow it. It should be in full sun during the warmer months, when it's fruiting, but it's okay if it receives less sun when it's dormant in winter. You can grow it in large pots or the garden.

When to grow it. It is best planted in winter, when it's dormant, but it can be planted at any time with care.

How to harvest. The tree will begin producing fruits about five years after planting. Pick the fruits as needed when they're red and before they start to split.

GRAPE

Vitis vinifera; Vitaceae (grape family)

Why grow it. This is a deciduous vine with the added bonus of edible fruits. Grow it in a sunny spot in the garden to provide shade in summer.

Where to grow it. Grow it over a trellis or pergola to suit your needs; you may want to plant two or three vines to ensure you get an even coverage. Do your research and discover the best way to prune a grapevine. We prune ours in winter to keep it manageable and producing grapes where we want them. More pruning may be necessary in summer to control wayward vines. They have low water requirements.

When to grow it. Buy the vine in winter, and plant it directly into the ground if you want to grow a large and robust vine. Fruit fly can be a problem, so prepare to manage this pest before you have them laying eggs in your grapes. You can buy ornamental varieties if you aren't fussed about eating the grapes.

How to harvest. Have a recipe ready, as the grapes will all ripen at around the same time. Cut the ripe bunches off the vine with secateurs, as close to the main vine as possible.

SAGE

Salvia officinalis; Lamiaceae (mint family)

Why grow it. A low-growing perennial herb, sage only grows to about 50 centimetres (20 inches) high. It can be grown in pots and garden beds, where it will spread out a little more.

Where to grow it. As with other hardy herbs, such as rosemary, thyme, lavender and oregano, sage prefers a location that offers full sun and dry conditions.

When to grow it. Sage can be planted any time of the year. Buy it in punnets, and plant a few seedlings around the garden in the sun.

How to harvest. Cut sage as needed with scissors, just removing some leaf tips from around the whole plant.

JALAPEÑO

Capsicum annuum; Solanaceae
(nightshade family)

Why grow it. This plant makes
anyone look like a rock-star
gardener! Our last jalapeño
plant gave us hundreds of
fruits, so we've learned to
make a mean hot sauce. It is
milder than a cayenne chilli,
so we like to add it more
generously to our cooking.
Where to grow it. Jalapeño
plants will be okay with half a
day's sun in a pot or garden
bed; they aren't too fussy. One
plant is definitely more than
enough for any family!
When to grow it. As with all
chilli plants, get your seedlings
into the soil in spring for an
autumn harvest.
How to harvest. Let your fruits
develop to a decent size, and then
pick them as required. Cut off the
fruits as close to the main stem
as possible.

CARROT

Daucus carota; Apiaceae
(carrot family)

Why grow it. Yes, carrots are
relatively cheap to buy, but you're
missing out on the excitement of
plucking a tastier version of these
root vegetables from the soil. You
can grow different types all year
round, so try a variety of colours
and sizes to suit your garden and
your tastebuds.
Where to grow it. Carrots need a
loose soil and aren't hungry feeders,
so keep the blood and bone at
bay. Garden beds will give the
longer varieties the depth they
need, but shorter or rounder
carrots will be fine in a pot with
a light mix. Carrots are okay in a
spot that gets half a day of sun.
When to grow it. Select carrot
seeds for the season in which you
want to grow them. Don't bother
buying carrot seedlings — just
prepare a light soil, plant your
seeds directly in the garden or

pot, cover them lightly with soil
and keep them moist. Pluck out
the weaker seedlings so the
strongest ones are spaced about
10 centimetres (4 inches) apart.
How to harvest. You'll be able to
see the coloured carrot tops poke
out of the soil as they get bigger.
Harvest the carrots when you can
see a decent-sized root growing
underneath, and plant more seeds
every eight weeks to keep the
carrots coming.

BEES AND HONEY

Among other things, having a
backyard hive means you have
access to an abundance of
sweet, golden liquid to use and
share. For us, the honey flows
into our morning chai, onto our
toast and into pretty much all of
our homemade desserts. You'll
notice in our recipes that our
go-to sweetener is always honey.
Feel free to replace this with your
sweetener of choice but, for us,
with plenty of the flavoursome

stuff produced by our backyard girls, we simply can't go past it. The frames of golden honeycomb produced in our hive are an art form in themselves. We often take a frame or two up to our local bakery for the community to share. If you've not yet got a hive, ask around your neighbourhood – chances are, someone's harvesting honey in your area. See if you can trade some of your freshly picked crops for a jar of honey so you can taste the delicious produce of your local honey bees.

LEMON

Citrus limon; Rutaceae (rue family)

Why grow it. Every backyard needs a citrus tree, and that's why many gardeners usually opt to plant a lemon tree before any other crops. 'Eureka', 'Lisbon', 'Lemonade' and the Meyer lemon are some well-known types. You can buy dwarf citrus varieties that suit pots and smaller spaces, but if you use lemons often, why not go for a standard-sized tree? You could keep it to around 4 metres (13 feet) x 3 metres (10 feet), and make it a feature of the yard.

Where to grow it. A lemon tree needs full sun and doesn't like root disturbance, so give it space out in the yard or even plant it in a large pot on its own. Remove dead or diseased branches as it grows, and keep the centre of the tree relatively open for sun and airflow.

When to grow it. As it's an evergreen tree, it's usually best to get it into the ground before the growing season begins. Late winter or early spring are the best times, so the tree can settle in before the heat of summer and make the most of the growing season. Keep it well watered during summer.

How to harvest. Cut off ripe lemons using secateurs, taking 5–10 centimetres (2–4 inches) of stem with each fruit.

LIME

Citrus latifolia; Rutaceae (rue family)

Why grow it. Depending on whether you grow it in a pot or the garden, this tree can reach between 1.5 metres (5 feet) and 4.5 metres (15 feet) in height. Ripe limes appear from autumn to winter. It's great to have the zest and acidity of a fresh lime for use in cooking.

Where to grow it. Place the tree in full sun. If you have the room, choose a regular-sized tree. If not, there are many dwarf types available. If you are using a pot, remember that the bigger the pot, the less likely the tree will dry out in the sun.

When to grow it. Spring is the best time but, with care, you can successfully plant the tree at any time of the year.

How to harvest. Cut off limes before they start turning yellow, using secateurs, and take a couple of centimetres of stem with each fruit.

Fermented jalapeño hot sauce

Makes 4 cups (1 litre/35 fl oz)

We're very lucky – our jalapeño bush is one of the most prolific plants in our garden. It produces more jalapeños than we could ever possibly consume. Fortunately for us, our neighbours are big fans of jalapeño hot sauce! This sauce is great for spicing up a simple ham sandwich or a Mexican fiesta. Add as many chillies as you like to bump up the heat rating.

Do

1 Place the water, vinegar, salt and honey into a large saucepan. Bring to the boil and then simmer over low heat for 5–10 minutes or until the salt has dissolved.

2 Fill a sterilised 4-cup (1-litre/35-fl-oz) jar with the jalapeños, onion and garlic cloves.

3 Pour the vinegar water into the jar, ensuring it covers the contents completely.

4 Place the lid on tightly. Leave the jar at room temperature for 1–2 weeks.

5 Once you're happy with the fermentation length, dispose of one-third of the liquid from the jar and pour the remaining mixture into a blender. Blend on high speed. Taste the mixture and add red chillies if necessary.

6 Strain the mixture through a fine-mesh sieve and into sterilised bottles. For a thick, spoonable sauce, pour the mixture into sterilised jars without straining.

7 The sauce will keep in the fridge for 10–12 weeks.

Use

2 cups (500 ml/17 fl oz) water

2 cups (500 ml/17 fl oz) vinegar

2 tablespoons salt

1 tablespoon honey

10–12 jalapeños (or enough to fill a 4-cup/1-litre/35-fl-oz jar almost to the top), chopped into quarters

½ white onion, sliced

4 garlic cloves

Red chillies (optional)

Oh and if you like your jalapeños really hot, let your plant's soil dry out a little when the fruits start appearing – this will encourage the fruits to produce more capsaicin. But don't let the plant wilt and die!

Coriander, lime and garlic dressing

Makes 2 cups (500 ml/17 fl oz)

This is our go-to salad dressing to accompany any bowl of leafy greens. With a tangy lime flavour, it will jazz up any old salad. The coriander is a must, but if you have an abundance of mint, feel free to add that in, too. And if you want a little extra creaminess, add a spoonful of tahini to the blend.

Do

1 Place all the ingredients into a blender or food processor and blend until smooth.
2 Pour the dressing into a sterilised jar and keep it in the fridge for up to 3 weeks.

Use

2 garlic cloves
55 g (2 oz) coriander (cilantro) leaves and stems, roughly chopped
Juice of 2 limes
3 tablespoons olive oil
2 tablespoons white wine vinegar
½ teaspoon sea salt

Feel free to serve the dressing in a dipping ramekin alongside torn pieces of freshly baked sourdough for a pre-dinner snack.

Rosemary and rocket pesto

Makes 1 cup (250 g/9 oz)

Who can resist a freshly baked loaf of warm sourdough with a thick layer of pesto? Not us! We are often found on a Sunday morning at our local bakery, tearing off handfuls of sourdough non-stop. It's a newsworthy day if our loaf makes it home in one piece! But for when it does make the journey home, we generally have a jar of this rosemary and rocket pesto waiting in our fridge to slather on the bread. Rosemary absolutely thrives in our garden; it's an easy herb to grow, and it adds a great flavour to any meal. The inclusion of rocket in this pesto makes for a peppery palate with a uniquely bright flavour.

Do

1 Strip the leaves from the rosemary stems and place them into a food processor with the other ingredients. Pulse until you achieve the desired texture (we like our pesto coarse and slightly crunchy).

2 Scoop the pesto into a sterilised jar and store the jar in the fridge for up to 2 weeks.

Use

6 large rosemary sprigs

2 cups (70 g/2½ oz) rocket (arugula) leaves

⅓ cup (50 g/1¾ oz) toasted pine nuts

½ cup (45 g/1½ oz) coarsely grated parmesan cheese

1 garlic clove

2 tablespoons freshly squeezed lemon juice

½ teaspoon sea salt

½ cup (125 ml/4 fl oz) olive oil (or macadamia oil, if you have it)

By the way, this recipe is also delicious if you replace the rocket leaves with lemon sorrel – just make sure you swap the lemon juice with extra olive oil, so that the pesto doesn't become too zesty!

Grape pizza *and* Pomegranate, apple cider and rosemary spritzer

Grape pizza

This recipe sounds a bit left of centre, but all the flavours work surprisingly well together.

Do

1 Preheat the oven to 180°C (350°F).

2 In a medium-sized bowl, mix together the warm water and yeast. Set it aside for 5–8 minutes or until it is foamy.

3 Add in 1 cup of flour and the salt, stirring with a spoon until the dough comes together but is still sticky.

4 Using your hands, on a floured surface, roll the dough into a ball. Knead the dough for 5 minutes or until it is smooth.

5 Rub the same bowl with olive oil and place the dough inside. Cover the bowl with a clean tea towel (dish towel) and put it in a warm place for 1–2 hours or until the dough has doubled in size (we sit ours on top of the fridge).

6 Meanwhile, in a small bowl, toss the grapes with the salt, pepper, 1 tablespoon of olive oil and the rosemary leaves. Place the mixture onto a baking tray and bake in the oven for 10–15 minutes or until the grape skins start to burst open. Remove the baking tray but leave the oven turned on.

7 Line a 37-cm (14½-in) diameter round baking tray with baking paper and then grease with olive oil.

8 Remove the dough from the bowl and add more flour (a tablespoon at a time) to alleviate the stickiness of the dough if necessary.

9 Place the dough onto the round baking tray. Pat out the dough evenly with your fingers and stretch it to the edge of the baking tray.

10 Top the dough with 1 tablespoon of olive oil and sprinkle with a pinch of salt.

11 Spread the cheeses and roasted grapes evenly over the dough.

12 Bake the pizza in the oven for 10–12 minutes or until the edges begin to lightly brown and the cheese topping starts to bubble.

Use

For the dough

1 cup (250 ml/9 fl oz) warm water

2 teaspoons dried yeast

3 cups (450 g/1 lb) plain (all-purpose) flour, divided into thirds

2 teaspoons salt

2 tablespoons olive oil

For the topping

2 cups (360 g/12¾ oz) seedless red grapes, halved lengthways

1 teaspoon sea salt

¼ teaspoon ground black pepper

2 tablespoons olive oil, divided in half

½ cup (25 g/1 oz) rosemary leaves

¼ cup (35 g/1¼ oz) coarsely grated gorgonzola cheese

¼ cup (25 g/1 oz) coarsely grated parmesan cheese

¼ cup (35 g/1¼ oz) coarsely grated mozzarella cheese

Oh and if you're in a hurry, opt for a store-bought pizza base – just be sure to get the freshest you can. Like most things in life, fresh is best.

Pomegranate, apple cider and rosemary spritzer

Serves 4

Autumn evenings call for more dinners inside, and less picnics outside. This spritzer is the perfect drink to kick off an evening with friends around the dinner table as the sun begins to set a little earlier. Freshly cut rosemary from the garden adds a subtle spiciness to the pomegranate and balances the sourness of the lime and cider.

Do

To make the rosemary syrup

1 Place the honey and water into a small saucepan over medium heat. Stir until the honey has dissolved. Add in 4 rosemary sprigs and leave on medium heat for another 2–3 minutes.

2 Remove the saucepan from the heat and let it stand for 30–40 minutes. Once the mixture is cool, discard the rosemary.

To make the spritzer

3 Pour the pomegranate seeds into a blender or food processor and blend until the seeds have a smoothie-like consistency. Strain through a fine-mesh strainer.

4 Pour the strained juice and the rosemary syrup into a cocktail shaker along with the lime juice and ice cubes. Shake vigorously.

5 Strain the mixture into four cocktail glasses and top up each with apple cider. Garnish with the remaining rosemary sprigs.

Use

¼ cup (90 g/3¼ oz) honey

½ cup (125 ml/4 fl oz) water

8 rosemary sprigs (about 10–15 cm/ 4–6 in long)

1½ cups (225 g/8 oz) pomegranate seeds

Juice of 1 lime

6 ice cubes

660 ml (22½ fl oz) alcoholic apple cider (we prefer the dry variety)

By the way, if you're lacking in the rosemary department, but excelling in the thyme, feel free to sub in the thyme for a slightly sweeter but still earthy flavour.

Rosemary and
sea salt flatbreads

If you ask us what our favourite snack is, we will most likely say cheese, dips and flatbread. We've even been known to call it a meal at least twice a week. The one challenge we've always faced with flatbreads, though, is the crazy ingredients they sneak into store-bought ones. We recently embarked on a mission to create our own healthy version, using only the good stuff. This recipe goes perfectly with freshly made guacamole or our smoky baba ghanoush on page 149. The only downside to these babies? They are insanely addictive (you have been warned!).

Do

1 Preheat the oven to 180°C (350°F). Line a baking tray with baking paper and then grease with olive oil.
2 Pat out the dough evenly with your fingers and stretch it to the edges of the baking tray. Cut it into 12 equal squares.
3 Heat 1 tablespoon of olive oil in a frying pan over medium heat.
4 Add the first four pieces of dough to the hot oil. They should sizzle a little. Cook each side until golden brown. Press down softly on the dough with a spatula to ensure even browning.
5 Move the flatbreads to a plate and sprinkle them with rosemary and sea salt. Repeat the process for the remaining batches, adding more olive oil to the frying pan if necessary.
6 Serve the flatbreads warm with a dip or two.

Use

Homemade pizza dough (see page 176)
⅓ cup (80 ml/2½ fl oz) olive oil
1 tablespoon fresh rosemary, chopped
1 heaped teaspoon sea salt flakes

Oh and if you skip the salt and top them with sesame seeds instead, these flatbreads can double as a great breakfast option.

Salted coriander and lime popcorn

Serves 4 as a snack

Growing coriander is often hit and miss, but when it's flourishing it goes great guns. With an abundance of the beautifully tasty greens growing in our garden, we've tried this herb in just about every kitchen concoction. We even snuck it into our popcorn and have never looked back. This popcorn is made with five simple ingredients and on the stovetop because we love the excitement of watching it go crazy.

Do

1 Place the coconut oil and a few kernels of popping corn into a large saucepan over medium–high heat.
2 As the coconut oil begins to melt, add in the coriander leaves.
3 Stay close by. Once the first kernel pops, add the sea salt to the melted coconut oil and pour in the rest of the kernels. Place the lid on the saucepan and grab the handle with an oven mitt. Shake the saucepan back and forth on the stovetop until the popping begins to slow. Remove the saucepan from the heat and crack open the lid slightly to allow the steam to escape.
4 Warm the lime juice and slowly pour it over the popcorn, trying to disperse the juice evenly without dampening any one area too much. Toss the popcorn with the lime zest and add salt to taste.
5 The popcorn will store in an airtight container at room temperature for 3–4 days.

Use

2 tablespoons coconut oil
⅓ cup (80 g/2¾ oz) popping corn
¼ cup (7 g/¼ oz) coriander (cilantro) leaves, finely chopped
¼ teaspoon sea salt flakes, plus extra to serve
Juice and zest of 1 lime

Oh and add some finely diced chilli if you want an extra kick.

Potato, sage and pecorino tarts

Makes 8 snack-sized pieces

As a kid, my mum used to whip up these tasty pastry tarts when friends would drop by last minute. The nostalgia of the scent of these cooking in the oven makes me impatient every time I prepare this recipe. Potato and sage are a perfect pairing for autumn evenings – they are warm, comforting and grounding.

Do

1 Preheat the oven to 180°C (350°). Line two baking trays with baking paper and then grease with olive oil.
2 Lay out the potato slices evenly on one of the baking trays and roast them in the oven for 15–20 minutes or until they are soft and beginning to brown. Remove them from the oven and set them aside.
3 In a small bowl, whisk the egg and olive oil together.
4 Place the puff pastry sheets onto the second baking tray. Brush with the egg and olive oil mixture.
5 Top the pastry sheets with potato slices, pecorino cheese, garlic and sage leaves. Season with salt and pepper to taste.
6 Place the pastry sheets into the oven and bake for 15 minutes or until the pecorino cheese has melted and the edges of the sheets are golden brown.
7 Garnish the pastry sheets with a few extra sage leaves. Slice the pastry into snack-sized pieces.

Use

450 g (1 lb) thinly sliced potatoes
1 egg
2 tablespoons olive oil
2 sheets (25 x 25 cm/10 x 10 in) frozen puff pastry, thawed
1 cup (100 g/3½ oz) grated pecorino cheese
2 garlic cloves, finely chopped
½ cup (10 g/¼ oz) sage leaves
Salt and freshly ground black pepper, to taste

Feel free to experiment with different toppings, as there are so many tastebud-winning combos!

Pomegranate and salted dark chocolate bark

Serves 4 as a snack

We were so happy when cacao came out of the woodwork as the superfood hero of recent years. Not that we needed an excuse to eat more chocolate! This recipe is our go-to dessert. The saltiness of the bark is a comforting and satisfying end to a delicious meal. Feel free to replace the pomegranate seeds with whatever you've got handy in the garden or pantry. The fun is in the experimentation.

Do

1 Line a baking tray with baking paper.
2 In a small saucepan over medium heat, melt the cacao butter and coconut oil until the mixture is runny and well combined.
3 Slowly add in the maple syrup and cacao powder and stir until the cacao powder has dissolved. Be careful not to overheat the mixture, as it can quickly burn.
4 Pour the mixture onto the baking tray. Sprinkle pomegranate seeds and sea salt flakes evenly over the mixture.
5 Place the baking tray into the freezer for 20 minutes or until the chocolate sets.
6 Break the chocolate into shards and serve.

Use

2 tablespoons cacao butter
1 tablespoon coconut oil
2 tablespoons maple syrup
2 tablespoons cacao powder
½ cup (75 g/2½ oz) pomegranate seeds
1 teaspoon sea salt flakes

Oh and it will keep in an airtight container in the freezer for 10–12 weeks.

Oregano and gingernut cookies

Makes 12 cookies

This recipe took a lot of testing and tweaking to finally get the perfect texture, but the result is a very close copy of your grandma's favourite crispy gingernut cookies that actually melt in your mouth. The crunchy texture and candied ginger are incredibly addictive! We store ours in the freezer to keep them fresh and crispy.

Do

1 Preheat the oven to 150°C (300°F). Line two baking trays with baking paper.
2 Place the cashews, desiccated coconut, ginger and oregano leaves into a food processor and blend until finely ground.
3 Pour the mixture into a medium-sized bowl. Stir through the cinnamon, bicarbonate of soda and sea salt.
4 Place the coconut oil, honey and lemon juice into a saucepan over low heat and stir until combined.
5 Pour the honey mixture into the cashew mixture and stir until combined.
6 Place spoonfuls of the mixture onto the baking trays, with a small gap between them.
7 Bake for 15 minutes or until the cookies are golden brown (the longer you bake them, the crispier they become).
8 Allow the cookies to cool on a wire rack before you eat them.

Use

¾ cup (120 g/4¼ oz) cashews (raw or roasted)
¼ cup (25 g/1 oz) desiccated (shredded) coconut
1 piece fresh ginger (5 x 3 cm/ 2 x 1¼ in), roughly chopped
¼ cup (7 g/¼ oz) fresh oregano leaves
1 teaspoon ground cinnamon
Pinch of bicarbonate of soda (baking soda)
½ teaspoon sea salt
2 tablespoons coconut oil
¼ cup (90 g/3¼ oz) honey
1 tablespoon freshly squeezed lemon juice

Feel free to replace the oregano with rosemary or thyme if you've got it growing.

Carrot and ginger
Japanese dressing

So much of our home-cooked food has a Japanese twist to it. We love the subtle flavours and crisp textures, as much as the perfectly crafted Japanese culture and lifestyle. One of the best things about visiting our favourite Japanese haunts is the crispy iceberg lettuce with that sweet and zesty carrot dressing drizzled on top. We love it so much we've been experimenting with making our own at home. And now, we can't stop adding it to everything!

Do

1 Place all the ingredients into a blender or food processor and blend until mostly smooth.

2 Taste the dressing and add salt and pepper if necessary.

3 Place the dressing into a sterilised jar and store the jar in the fridge for up to 3 weeks.

Use

6 carrots (tops removed), peeled and roughly chopped

2 tablespoons grated fresh ginger

1 garlic clove

¼ cup (60 ml/2 fl oz) rice vinegar

2 tablespoons tahini

2 tablespoons soy sauce

2 tablespoons toasted sesame oil

Juice of ½ orange

Salt and freshly ground black pepper, to taste

Oh and this dressing goes perfectly with baked fish or a simple cucumber salad.

Lemon curd with mint

Makes 2 cups (500 ml/17 fl oz)

We have a bakery just around the corner that does the best sourdough in the world. We often take up a jar of this lemon curd to trade for a loaf of the heavenly bread. Have a jar of this citrus treat on hand all year round so you can slather it on toast whenever the mood strikes you. The mint adds a bright zing to this luscious spread.

Do

1 In a medium saucepan, bring the water to a simmer over medium heat.
2 In a metal bowl, whisk the yolks, sugar and honey vigorously until the mixture is smooth. Add the lemon juice and salt. Whisk again.
3 Once the water reaches a simmer, reduce the heat to low and place the metal bowl over the saucepan (don't let the water touch the base of the bowl).
4 Cook the mixture, whisking constantly, for about 20 minutes or until it has thickened. The mixture should be thick enough to coat the back of a wooden spoon but still runny enough to pour. Do not allow the mixture to boil, or it will curdle.
5 Remove the bowl from the heat and whisk in the lemon zest and mint. Add the butter gradually, one cube at a time, whisking well to combine. Allow each cube of butter to melt completely before adding more.
6 Let the curd cool in the bowl at room temperature for 1 hour. Cover the bowl with plastic wrap and refrigerate overnight.
7 The next morning, give the curd a whisk to make sure it's smooth, then transfer it into sterilised jars. Serve and enjoy!

Use

½ cup (125 ml/4 fl oz) water
8 egg yolks
1 cup (220 g/7¾ oz) coconut sugar (or granulated sugar)
2 tablespoons honey
Juice of 4 lemons
Pinch of salt
1 tablespoon finely grated lemon zest
¼ cup (15 g/½ oz) finely sliced mint leaves
125 g (4½ oz) unsalted butter, cut into cubes

Remember to hide this one at the back of the fridge, because it will get gobbled up quick smart.

Winter

Plants: Thyme / Turmeric / Orange / Ginger / Beetroot / Rainbow chard / Kale / Bok choy / English spinach / Cabbage

Recipes: Polenta chips with thyme aïoli / Turmeric flu shot / Spicy pickled rainbow chard / Beetroot and chilli sauce / Alcoholic ginger beer with honey from the hive / Cabbage and beetroot sauerkraut / Sticky ginger chai / Kale, lime and sesame crackers / Miso, orange and tahini sauce / Japanese-style bok choy salad / English spinach and chive pancakes / Chocolate, orange and pistachio salami / Upside-down blood orange and turmeric cake

When the cooler air creeps under our doors, we wrap ourselves up and dream of summer getaways. The deciduous trees have shed their leaves, and our teapot barely has the chance to cool down between brews. The garden is full of plants that developed during the warmer seasons and will be our food supply for the next few months. As the days begin to rapidly shorten towards the winter solstice, snuggly woollens make a welcome return.

In our household, winter sees an even greater focus on food. We spend more time indoors, and our bodies crave extra nourishment. Winter is not a doing time. It's a thinking time and a planning time. We often find ourselves gazing at our garden, steaming hot coffee in hand, dreaming up new ideas for the coming seasons. What will we do differently? How can we improve the garden?

Towards the end of winter, we order our seeds and prepare our garden beds or pots for planting the seeds in spring. We harvest some of the herbaceous perennials, such as ginger and turmeric, to keep us lively and kicking on through the cooler months.

Winter is a great time to prune your deciduous fruit trees and vines. Pomegranate, fig and grape, for example, can be pruned if required to remove dead wood and crossing branches; this opens up the canopy to allow in more light and airflow, and promotes the growth of fruits where you want them to appear on the branches. Keeping your fruit trees and vines at a manageable shape and size is good horticultural practice. Pruning timing and techniques vary between species, so do some research before making any cuts.

Hopefully your garden is in sun at this time of year, as it's delightful to be outside in the bracing air, harvesting goodies throughout winter. It's slow growing in the garden, though, so take some time to relax and enjoy yourself, cook good meals and observe the wonders of the winter season.

Winter Plants.

THYME

Thymus vulgaris; Lamiaceae
(mint family)

Why grow it. Thyme makes for an attractive, fast-growing ground cover. Ours runs around the base of our lemon tree, trails down our stairs and sneaks over the path – it's such a beautiful edible plant that works well as an ornamental, too. With its rich, earthy flavour, thyme is the perfect addition to meat dishes or roasted vegetables, and it's an ideal garnish for a variety of winter soups.

Where to grow it. Grow thyme in the sunniest spot in the garden. Pots and garden beds are fine, but not if the thyme is going to get watered every day along with your thirsty vegetables. Don't use pots with saucers or self-watering pots, as these will keep your thyme too moist. Grow thyme, rosemary, sage, oregano and lavender in the same hot, dry conditions, or you'll give them wet feet and cause fungal problems.

When to grow it. Buy thyme in small punnets – there are many different varieties from which to choose – and plant the seedlings during spring. I think the original garden thyme is the most robust and best tasting.

How to harvest. Snip the ends of stems whenever you need some thyme for the kitchen. This helps to promote a bushy, low plant habit.

TURMERIC

Curcuma longa; Zingiberaceae
(ginger family)

Why grow it. People are often surprised when we tell them we grow our own turmeric, but it's actually one of the least fussy edible plants we've ever grown. Once you plant it, you can almost forget about it. And the best part is you use it so sparingly in the kitchen that you don't need to grow stacks of it. The tiniest spoonful adds a strong burst of flavour to your dish. When we're fighting off a head cold, we love to blend it with some greens to make a super juice that helps our immune system.

Turmeric.

From left to right

Beetroot (beets),
oranges and ginger.

Where to grow it. Similar to ginger, this herbaceous perennial has large, strappy, green leaves and flowers that suit a tropical-style garden. Bury the turmeric rhizomes about 5 centimetres (2 inches) deep.

When to grow it. You can plant the rhizomes in the garden or pots during spring.

How to harvest. Lift and divide the rhizomes during winter when the plant is dormant. Split them up, use some for cooking and replant the others in the garden or in pots.

ORANGE

Citrus sinensis; Rutaceae
(rue family)

Why grow it. We love orange trees in gardens for the bright pops of colour they add to a usually green-washed background. The orange is a versatile fruit with a bold flavour – not only is it delicious to eat straight off the tree, but it's also a beautiful ingredient to add to desserts, sauces and your freshly squeezed juice.

Where to grow it. Grow it in a large pot or container, or right in the middle of the yard as a feature tree.

When to grow it. When you have found the right location in the garden, start looking for an attractive specimen. If you want instant fruits and size, you can buy established trees that are already more than 2 metres (6½ feet) in height. The same goes for most citrus trees – nurseries can get in advanced specimens. Plant your orange tree at any time of the year with care.

How to harvest. Harvest oranges when they are ripe in autumn and winter. Take care of your fruit trees with pruning, and ensure they have adequate nutrients and water during the year. Keep an open canopy to allow in good airflow and sunlight.

GINGER

Zingiber officinale; Zingiberaceae
(ginger family)

Why grow it. I like to grow our own ginger (along with galangal),

so we always have fresh ginger rhizomes handy for our kitchen needs. The strappy green leaves make the plant look like a mini corn crop about 40 centimetres (16 inches) high.

Where to grow it. Grow ginger anywhere that receives a half day to full day of sun, and keep the soil fairly moist.

When to grow it. You can plant the rhizomes in the garden or pots during early spring.

How to harvest. Lift and divide the rhizomes during winter when the plant is dormant. Split them up, use some for cooking and replant the others around the garden or in pots.

BEETROOT (BEET)

Beta vulgaris; Amaranthaceae
(amaranth family)

Why grow it. This vegie comes in an array of colours and sizes, plus you can use the young leaves in salads, too.

From left to right

Rainbow chard, bok choy and kale.

Where to grow it. Grow it in the garden with full sun, and space the plants about 10 centimetres (4 inches) apart.

When to grow it. Grow from seed, and then thin out the seedlings. Plant quite a few successions of beetroot over the growing season from late winter through to the following autumn.

How to harvest. Most types will be ready to harvest ten weeks after sowing. Use some of the young shoots for salads while you wait for the mature edible taproots to form.

RAINBOW CHARD

Beta vulgaris; Amaranthaceae (amaranth family)

Why grow it. Rainbow chard is always a favourite with the kids, not just for its bright colours but also because it is an easy, rewarding plant to grow. As the name suggests, the rainbow-coloured stalks do a brilliant job of cheering up your winter garden. The stalks are crunchy when eaten raw in a salad, but, in our books, they are even better when pickled. The leaves are full and hearty, and they are best eaten after being lightly sautéed.

Where to grow it. Rainbow chard isn't too fussy, as long as it gets a half day to a full day of sun – grow it wherever you have the space.

When to grow it. Grow from seed in spring and autumn, and enjoy the plant for up to 18 months.

How to harvest. Cut off the outside leaves as you need them, but always leave some inner leaves so the plant can keep powering on. Trim off dead or yellow leaves around the base, so you have a clean stalk with healthy leaves only.

KALE

Brassica oleracea; Brassicaceae (mustard family)

Why grow it. Kale is the powerhouse of the salad greens in our garden. It's a hardy plant that comes in a range of varieties and flavours. As well as bulking up any salad, it is also the ultimate addition to your green smoothie.

Where to grow it. Kale will grow well in large pots, raised beds and planters with good sun. It's a strong plant that will provide greens for you throughout the year if it has room to grow. It can grow to waist height, so plant it towards the back of the garden where it won't shade your other plants.

When to grow it. We like growing Tuscan kale, which is the dark green–blue type. Plant it in spring, and it will often give you a good year of growth before flowering.

How to harvest. Simply cut off the lower leaves, working your way upwards – never cut through the stem or top young leaves.

BOK CHOY

Brassica rapa; Brassicaceae (mustard family)

Why grow it. Quick-turnover Asian greens – such as bok choy,

tatsoi and mizuna – allow you to keep something growing in the garden for most of the year in warmer climates.

Where to grow it. Bok choy can be grown anywhere with at least half a day's sun. If you're not fussed about the type of Asian greens you grow, you can get a packet of mixed seeds and see what comes out.

When to grow it. Have a go at growing a variety of Asian greens from seed at any time of the year.

How to harvest. Cut off bok choy at the base, and bring the whole plant to the kitchen. Use succession planting to maintain your supply.

ENGLISH SPINACH

Spinacia oleracea; Amaranthaceae (amaranth family)

Why grow it. English spinach is a trusty old favourite in the garden. It's a nutrient-dense leafy green that grows quickly in the right conditions. We love adding it to our repertoire of winter pie recipes, because the health benefits of English spinach provide an excuse for us to eat as much pastry as we can!

Where to grow it. English spinach copes well in both garden beds and large pots.

When to grow it. The peak time for growing English spinach is the end of summer through to winter.

How to harvest. Cut off the outside leaves as you need them, but always leave some inner leaves so the plant can keep powering on. Trim off dead or yellow leaves around the base, so you have a clean stalk with healthy leaves only.

CABBAGE

Brassica oleracea; Brassicaceae (mustard family)

Why grow it. We grow the late-season 'Red Drumhead' variety to make sauerkraut. We plant these at the end of summer or in autumn, and they take a few months to form a dense head.

Where to grow it. Cabbages and other cool-season brassicas – such as collard greens, cauliflower, broccoli and brussels sprouts – are best placed in garden beds with plenty of room for full sun and airflow around them.

When to grow it. Plant seedlings in autumn, and keep an eye out for cabbage moths and caterpillars.

How to harvest. Use your knife to cut through the base at ground level when the purplish red head is tight and dense.

Collard greens.

Polenta chips with thyme aïoli

Although we crave comfort food in winter, it doesn't have to be naughty. This is our go-to snack for an afternoon with good friends and good beer. These chips feature a crispy outer crust and a soft, pillowy inside. The thyme aïoli has a subtle woody flavour and is also an ideal addition to a ham and cheese toasted sandwich.

Do

1 Grease a 20-cm (8-in) square cake tin with olive oil.

2 In a medium saucepan, bring the vegie stock to the boil. Slowly pour in the polenta, while whisking to prevent the polenta from clumping. Continue to whisk for 2–3 minutes or until the mixture has thickened.

3 Remove the saucepan from the heat and stir in the parmesan cheese, butter and thyme. Add salt and pepper to taste.

4 Pour the polenta mixture into the cake tin and allow it to cool. Once cool, place plastic wrap directly onto the surface of the polenta to smother it. Place the cake tin into the fridge for about 2 hours or until the polenta is completely set and cold.

5 Preheat the oven to 200°C (400°F). Line a baking tray with baking paper.

6 Turn out the block of polenta onto a chopping board and use a knife to slice it into thick chips.

7 Place the chips onto the baking tray. Drizzle with olive oil and toss gently to coat all sides. Sprinkle with some sea salt flakes. Bake the chips in the oven for 25–35 minutes or until they are golden and crispy.

8 To make the aïoli, place the roasted garlic, egg, thyme, lemon juice, apple cider vinegar, salt and pepper into a food processor and blend until smooth. Pour the mixture into a small mixing bowl and slowly add the olive oil, whisking until it is fully emulsified. Chill the aïoli in the fridge.

9 Serve the chips hot alongside a dipping bowl with the cold aïoli.

Use

For the polenta chips

4 cups (1 litre/35 fl oz) quality vegie stock

1 cup (190 g/6¾ oz) fine (instant) polenta (cornmeal)

½ cup (50 g/1¾ oz) finely grated parmesan cheese

2 tablespoons butter

2 tablespoons finely chopped thyme

Sea salt and cracked black pepper, to taste

2–3 tablespoons olive oil

Sea salt flakes, to taste

For the aïoli

4–6 garlic cloves (roasted in a 200°C /400°F oven for 15 minutes or until tender)

1 large egg

1 tablespoon finely chopped thyme

1 tablespoon lemon juice

2 teaspoons apple cider vinegar

Salt and freshly ground black pepper, to taste

½ cup (125 ml/4 fl oz) olive oil

Oh and if you love a herby flavour, add rosemary or oregano to the polenta when you stir in the parmesan cheese.

Turmeric flu shot

It's at this time of year that we feel a little slow and our immune system often takes a hit. At home, we make our own flu shot remedy to keep the germs at bay. Although it is super-hard to swallow, you'll have to trust us that this concoction does the trick. Store the remedy in your fridge and have a shot every night before bed until the jar is empty and you're feeling fresh.

Do

1 Place the garlic, ginger, cayenne pepper, lemon juice, honey, dandelion root, turmeric and water into a saucepan over low heat. Let the mixture simmer for 5–10 minutes.

2 Place the mixture into the fridge to cool.

3 If you've got it on hand, add some apple cider vinegar, vitamin C powder and liquid zinc to the cooled mixture.

4 Pour about 20 ml (½ fl oz) of the remedy into a small glass, hold your nose and scull!

Use

3 garlic cloves, finely chopped

3 cm (1¼ in) fresh ginger knob, finely chopped

¼ teaspoon cayenne pepper

Juice of 1 lemon

1 teaspoon honey

1 teaspoon dandelion root, finely chopped

½ teaspoon turmeric powder

½ cup (125 ml/4 fl oz) water

If you're really in need

¼ cup (60 ml/2 fl oz) apple cider vinegar

2 teaspoons vitamin C powder

Dash of liquid zinc

By the way, we'd recommend chasing down the remedy with some juice or kombucha. The flavour is very strong!

Spicy pickled rainbow chard

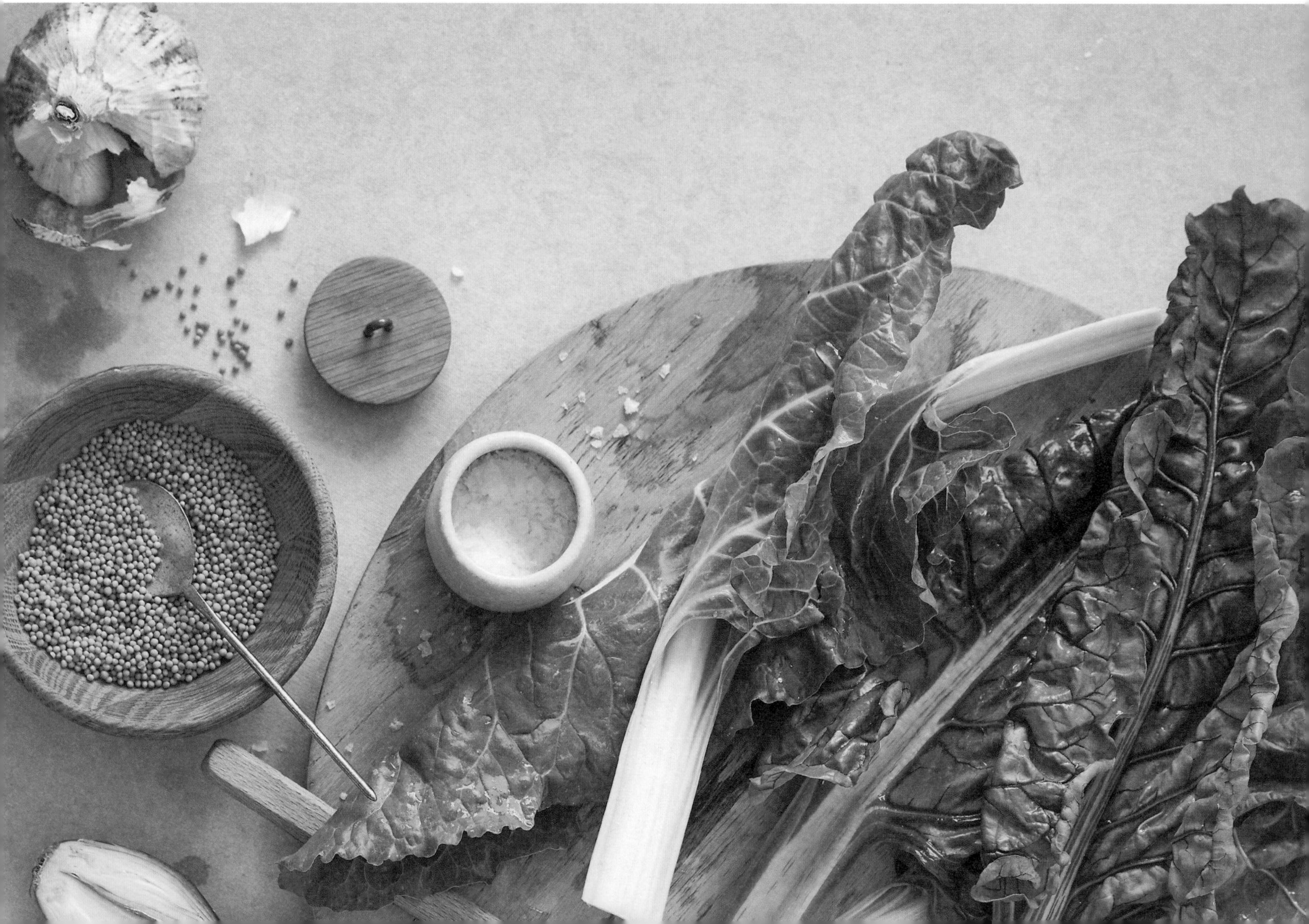

Spicy pickled rainbow chard

Makes 1 kg (2 lb 4 oz)

Here's something a little bit different – it's slightly spicy, vibrantly colourful and a whole lot of fun. One thing we try to do with the plants we grow is appreciate each and every part of their creation. We try to practise root to leaf eating, so that nothing is wasted. It means that we are more creative in the kitchen and less wasteful overall. These pickled chard stems are a colourful snack to add to a ploughman's board. We always seem to preserve more than we can eat! Don't discard the beautiful rich green leaves – these are a nutrient-dense addition to a salad or can be lightly sautéed with your morning eggs.

Do

1 Cut the rainbow chard stems to fit in sterilised jars and place them into two jars.

2 Place 1 garlic clove into each jar.

3 In a small saucepan, bring to the boil the vinegars, honey and salt. Stir until the honey and salt have dissolved.

4 Remove the saucepan from the heat and stir in the shallot, mustard seeds and chilli. Pour the mixture over the rainbow chard stems and garlic, ensuring that the shallot, mustard seeds and chilli are evenly dispersed between the two jars. Allow the mixture to cool.

5 Place a lid on each jar and store the jars in the fridge for 2–3 weeks.

6 The pickled rainbow chard stems will be ready to eat after they have been in the fridge for 2 days.

Use

340 g (12 oz) rainbow chard stems, leaves removed

2 garlic cloves

½ cup (125 ml/4 fl oz) white wine vinegar

½ cup (125 ml/4 fl oz) rice vinegar

3 tablespoons honey

1½ teaspoons salt

½ French shallot, thinly sliced

½ teaspoon mustard seeds

½ teaspoon thinly sliced chilli

Remember to keep a jar on hand so you have a ready-made present for a foodie friend!

Beetroot and chilli sauce

Makes 4 cups (1 litre/35 fl oz)

Unlike most sauces on the supermarket shelves, this one has zero refined sugar and zero preservatives. It's a delicious addition to your burgers, barbecued meats or morning egg and bacon roll. The beetroot provides a lovely colour, earthiness and sweetness, and is perfectly balanced by the vibrancy of the chilli. And the best part is that beetroot is really easy to grow!

Do

1 Preheat the oven to 180°C (350°F). Line a baking tray with foil.
2 Place the beetroot, red onion and garlic clove onto the baking tray. Drizzle with 2 tablespoons of olive oil, sprinkle with salt and pepper, and wrap the foil around the vegies. Bake for 1 hour or until the beetroot are tender on the inside. Set the vegies aside and allow them to cool.
3 In a small saucepan, heat the remaining oil over medium heat. Add the celery and cook for 10 minutes or until it has softened. Stir in the cumin, paprika, chilli, salt, vinegar and honey. Cover and gently simmer for a further 5–10 minutes. Remove the saucepan from the heat and allow it to cool.
4 Place the beetroot mixture and the celery mixture into a food processor and blend for 3–4 minutes or until the sauce is completely smooth.
5 Pour the sauce into sterilised bottles and store the bottles in the fridge. The sauce will keep for up to 2 weeks.

Use

5 medium beetroot (beets), washed, peeled and cut into wedges
1 red onion, peeled and chopped into wedges
1 garlic clove
4 tablespoons olive oil, divided in half
Salt and freshly ground black pepper, to taste
1 celery stalk, diced
½ teaspoon ground cumin
½ teaspoon mild paprika
1 fresh red chilli, finely chopped
½ teaspoon salt
200 ml (7 fl oz) apple cider vinegar
2 teaspoons honey

Oh and if you prefer a sauce with less heat, remove the seeds from your chillies before adding them to the saucepan.

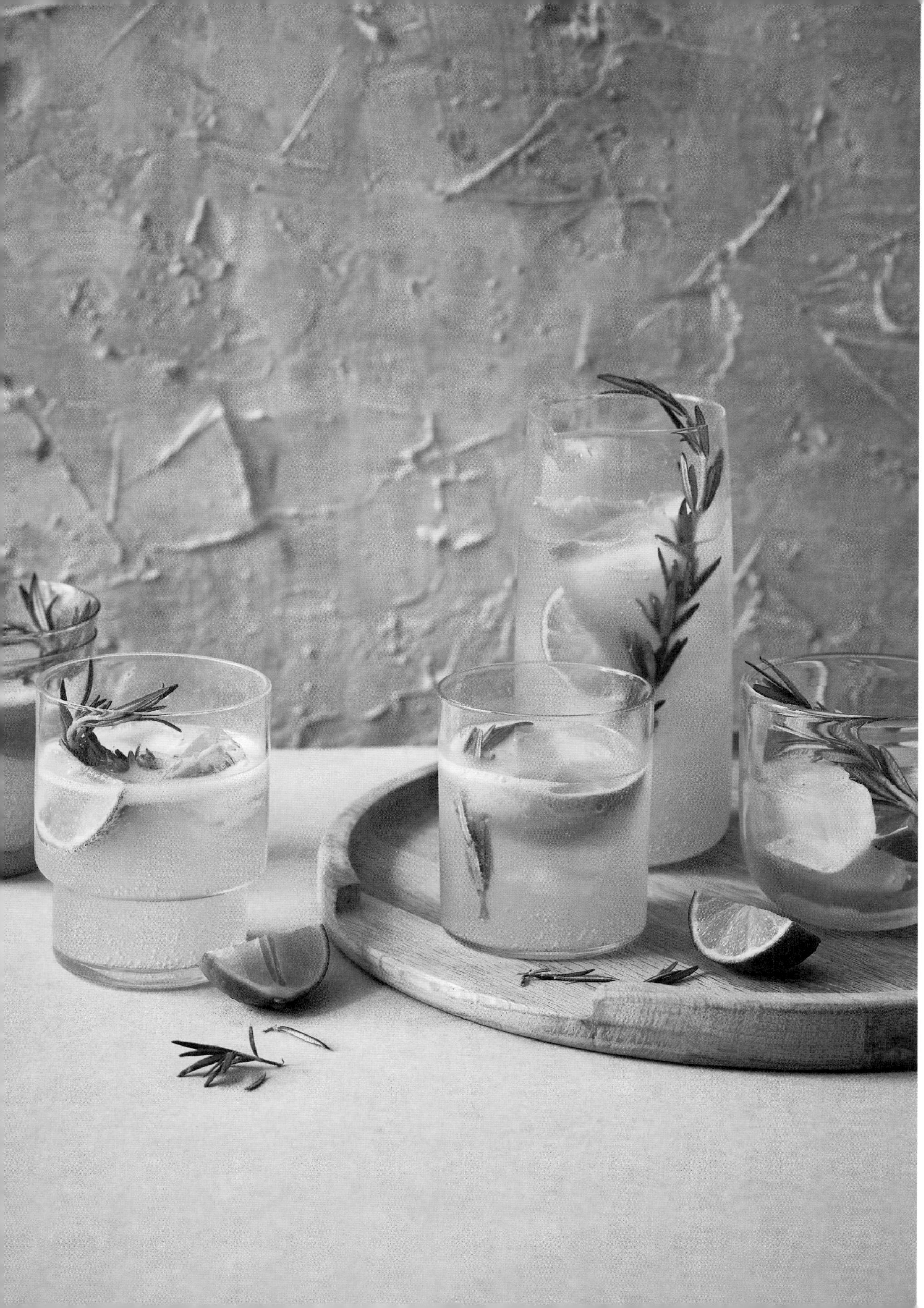

Alcoholic ginger beer with honey from the hive

Alcoholic ginger beer with honey from the hive

Makes about 20 cups (5 litres/175 fl oz)

Our hive produces on average about 1 kg (2 lb 4 oz) of honey per week. What do we do with our liquid gold? We trade it, of course! We give our dear friend Katie some honey, and she gives us a few big bottles of ginger beer – and we couldn't be happier. This is her tried and tested recipe for the best ginger beer you will ever taste. It is one of the more complex recipes in this book, but don't be disheartened – the amount of effort you put in will be well worth it when you are sipping your refreshing ginger beer as you while away the hours in your winter garden.

Do

Preparing the ginger culture

1 Place 1 cup (250 ml/9 fl oz) of water and the ginger into a food processor and blend until the mixture is pulpy. Set the mixture aside.

2 In a large sterilised jar, stir the yeast into 1 cup (250 ml/ 9 fl oz) of warm water until it has dissolved. Add 1 tablespoon of ginger pulp, 1 tablespoon of honey, the lemon juice and the sliced jalapeño (if you're using it). Tighten the lid and shake the jar vigorously.

3 Remove the jar lid. Cover the neck of the jar with a clean, dry tea towel (dish towel) and secure it with a rubber band. Put the jar in the warmest place in your house: next to your heater, on top of the fridge or in a sunny spot on the bench.

Use

20 cups (5 litres/175 fl oz) unchlorinated water, divided

3 cups (600 g/1 lb 5 oz) peeled and coarsely chopped fresh ginger

1½ teaspoons champagne yeast (find it at your local brewing store)

1 kg (2 lb 4 oz) honey

Juice of 2 lemons

1 jalapeño, seeds removed, sliced (optional)

Lime wedges, to serve

Ice cubes, to serve

Rosemary sprigs, to serve

4 Every day for the next week, you'll need to 'feed' your culture. Firstly, feel the jar with your hands – it should be lukewarm. If it's too cold, your yeast will go into hibernation and stop doing its thing, and if it's too hot your yeast might perish. Remove the tea towel (dish towel) and add 1 tablespoon of ginger pulp and 1 tablespoon of honey. Tighten the jar lid and shake the jar vigorously. Remove the jar lid and cover the jar with the tea towel (dish towel) again. Put your jar back in its warm place to brew.

5 After feeding your ginger culture for a week, you should see small bubbles floating to the surface of your culture.

Bottling your brew

1 Using a funnel, fill three clean plastic bottles (not glass bottles, which may explode!) two-thirds of the way up with warm water. Divide the remaining honey among the plastic bottles, screw on the bottle caps and shake the bottles vigorously to dissolve the honey.

2 Using muslin (cheesecloth) or a fine-mesh strainer, strain the culture out into a large measuring cup. Divide the culture evenly among the plastic bottles – there should be enough to add about 250 ml (9 fl oz/1 cup) of the culture liquid to each plastic bottle. Gently rock the bottles back and forth to combine. Now's the time to dip in a finger and taste the ginger beer. If you want your ginger beer to be stronger, add more culture liquid; if you want it less intense, add more lukewarm water.

3 Screw on the bottle caps tightly and store the bottles in the same warm place you kept your ginger culture. Gently squeeze the bottles each day to test how they're carbonating.

4 After 3–4 days, they should become difficult to squeeze. When they feel solid and are impossible to squeeze at all, slowly start to unscrew the bottle caps until you hear hissing, but do not open them all the way. Whenever the bottle is impossible to squeeze, let out some of the carbonation and then screw the bottle cap back on tightly.

5 In about 12–14 days, the yeast should have eaten up most of the sugar (honey) in the bottle. Unfortunately, there's no sign to let you know if this is done – you've got to go by intuition and a bit of trial and error. Start by first testing one bottle and see what that one tastes like before opening up the other two.

6 Serve the ginger beer with lime wedges, loads of ice and a rosemary sprig.

By the way, we'd definitely recommend throwing a party to show off your phenomenal brewing skills.

Cabbage and beetroot sauerkraut

Makes about 1.5 kg (3 lb 5 oz)

This is our daily addiction, and the one thing we crave when away from home! It has just the right balance of crunchiness and softness, saltiness and sweetness, and the seeds and capers make for a beautiful texture. We add it to everything: breakfast, lunch and dinner. It provides every meal with colour and vibrancy, and, what's more, it's amazing for your health.

Do

1 In a large bowl, mix the cabbage, beetroot, fennel, dill and salt. Use your hands to firmly massage the mixture for 5–10 minutes or until the vegetable juices start to collect in the bottom of the bowl.

2 Add the capers and seeds to the mixture and stir well, again with your hands.

3 Place the mixture into two large sterilised jars and press it down into each jar so that it is as compact as it can be. Leave a 5 cm (2 in) gap at the top of each jar. The juices should rise and cover the mixture.

4 Place a lid on each jar and let the jars sit at room temperature for 2–3 weeks or until the sauerkraut tastes tangy and somewhat sour.

5 Store the sauerkraut in the fridge for up to 12 weeks. Serve it with salads, sandwiches, scrambled eggs and just about anything else to add some gut-healing deliciousness to your meal.

Use

½ red cabbage, chopped

½ white cabbage, chopped

4 beetroot (beets), peeled and grated

2 fennel bulbs (remove tough outer layer), chopped

4 dill sprigs, chopped

4 tablespoons fine sea salt

⅓ cup (60 g/2¼ oz) baby capers, rinsed

1 tablespoon caraway seeds

1 tablespoon fennel seeds

1 tablespoon sesame seeds

Feel free to experiment with other vegies from the garden, as long as they are firm and robust enough to retain their shape and texture throughout the fermentation process. Just be sure to keep the same ratio of vegetable to salt to ensure the process is a success.

Sticky ginger chai

Whenever we go camping, we pack our gas cooker, enamel teapot and a jar of homemade chai. Waking up to the smell of this delicious tea brings back so many memories of deserted beaches, epic waves and warm sunrises. Our kelpie even loves to eat the leftover brew. This chai mix is full of warming spices and has an earthy, sweet flavour that wakes up the sleepiest of heads.

Do

1 Place all the spices into a mortar and grind with a pestle for 1–2 minutes to release the flavours.
2 Combine the tea, fresh ginger and spices in a small mixing bowl. Slowly pour the honey over the top while continuously stirring the mixture to ensure the ingredients are evenly coated with honey.
3 Place the mixture into a sterilised jar and store the jar in the fridge for up to 4–6 weeks. Make the chai with hot water and milk of your choice.

Use

16 cardamom pods
3 cinnamon sticks
1 teaspoon freshly grated nutmeg
1 teaspoon fennel seeds
1 teaspoon coriander seeds
8 cloves
2 star anise
1 teaspoon black peppercorns
1½ tablespoons black tea leaves
    (use a quality Ceylon tea for a
    more robust flavour)
2 tablespoons thinly sliced fresh
    ginger
2 tablespoons honey
Milk, to serve

Oh and if you're feeling a winter cold coming on, add 1 tablespoon of freshly grated turmeric as well.

Kale, lime and sesame crackers

Makes 25–30 crackers

The cosiness of winter means snacking, snacking and more snacking. We often find ourselves clinging to the pantry doors in search of a little something to satisfy our bellies. These tasty crackers are always just what we're looking for! They are just as good on their own as they are with a lashing of dip. The addition of kale and lime elevates the usual sesame crackers into a powerhouse of nutrients and taste.

Do

1 Preheat the oven to 180°C (350°F). Line two baking trays with baking paper.
2 Place the nuts, kale and garlic into a food processor and blend until the mixture becomes fine and grainy. Pour the mixture into a medium-sized mixing bowl and add the egg, lime juice, oil and sea salt. Using a wooden spoon, stir the mixture until it comes together as a dough.
3 Divide the dough in two and place each half onto a baking tray. Using a rolling pin, roll the dough out evenly on the baking trays. If the dough sticks to the rolling pin, place another piece of baking paper between the dough and the rolling pin. Use a knife to slice the flat dough into squares.
4 Sprinkle sesame seeds on top of the dough and place the baking trays into the oven for 10–12 minutes. Be sure to keep an eye on the dough, as it tends to burn quite easily.

Use

2 cups (280 g/10 oz) raw mixed nuts (we use cashews and almonds)
1 cup (70 g/2½ oz) kale, ribs removed
1 garlic clove
1 egg
1 tablespoon freshly squeezed lime juice
1 tablespoon olive oil
1 teaspoon sea salt
¼ cup (40 g/1½ oz) sesame seeds

By the way, for a fresh hit, add a small handful of coriander (cilantro) leaves to the food processor if you've got this herb growing in the garden.

Miso, orange and tahini sauce

Makes 2 cups (500 ml/17 fl oz)

You know those sauces that you stumble across and think, 'Man, this is so good – I'm going to put it on everything from now on!'? Yeah, well this is one of those guys. It's sweet enough to slather atop a chocolate cake, but savoury enough to drizzle on your salad. Our favourite thing is to spread it generously over eggplant halves before popping them into the oven and watching the sauce glaze over. For us, citrus trees are a must-have plant in any garden. The sweet yet acidic juice of the fruit is a chef's best friend at every meal, from breakfast through to dinner and on to dessert.

Do

1 Place the whole orange into a medium-sized saucepan of boiling water and boil for 1.5–2 hours or until it is soft enough for a skewer to go through with ease. Top up the water from time to time so that the orange is always fully submerged. Spin the orange around occasionally so that it cooks through evenly. When it is ready, drain the orange and leave it to cool.
2 Chop the cooled orange into wedges and remove any pips. Place the orange, tahini and miso paste into a food processor and blend until smooth.
3 Place the mixture into a sterilised jar and store the jar in the fridge for up to 3 weeks.

Use

1 orange, skin on
2 tablespoons tahini
1 tablespoon white miso paste

Oh and when it's in season, try replacing the standard orange with a blood orange – the flavour is really something else.

Japanese-style bok choy salad

Serves 4 as a side dish

Bok choy is one of the easiest Asian greens to grow. Ours often all spring up at once, though, and we are left to madly find ways of cooking and devouring its lush and buttery leaves. One of our favourite ways to cook it is hot and fast, with a nutty Japanese twist. This recipe is the ideal side dish to accompany a warming winter meal of soba noodles or brown rice.

Do

1 In a small bowl, mix the mirin, miso paste, rice vinegar and lime juice together until the miso has completely dispersed.

2 In a medium saucepan, heat 1 tablespoon of peanut oil over high heat. Add the garlic and ginger and stir for 30 seconds, then add the miso mixture and cook for about 1 minute; the mixture should thicken up slightly. Remove the saucepan from the heat and stir in the sesame oil.

3 In a large frying pan, heat 1 tablespoon of peanut oil over high heat. Add the bok choy and cook for about 5 minutes or until the outer edges of the stalks start to brown and crisp up.

4 Remove the frying pan from the heat. Place the bok choy onto serving plates and drizzle the miso mixture over the top. Sprinkle with cashews, sesame seeds and chilli flakes. Serve immediately, while the bok choy is still hot and crispy.

Use

½ cup (125 ml/4 fl oz) mirin (rice wine)

1 heaped tablespoon white miso paste

1 tablespoon rice vinegar

Juice of ½ lime

2 tablespoons peanut oil, divided in half

1 garlic clove, sliced on a mandoline

1 teaspoon grated fresh ginger

2½ tablespoons sesame oil

4 bok choy bulbs, sliced in half lengthways

⅓ cup (50 g/1¾ oz) roasted cashews, finely chopped

1 teaspoon black sesame seeds

Chilli flakes, to taste

By the way, if you want to get a little adventurous in the garden, you could try your hand at growing some Chinese broccoli (gai lan) to use in this recipe.

English spinach and chive pancakes

Deciding what to eat for breakfast is a very serious and frequent topic of discussion in our house. I'm a bit of a savoury fiend myself, but Tess is obsessed with pancakes. And so, as all good couples do, we learned to compromise with this English spinach and chive pancake recipe. This is the ideal comforting breakfast food when it's too cold for cereal, but you're sick of eating porridge. Best of all, English spinach is easy to grow and packed with nutrients.

Do

1 Place the flour and baking powder into a large mixing bowl and slowly pour in the water while stirring with an egg whisk. Once combined, whisk in the egg.
2 Stir in the English spinach, chives, soy sauce, sesame oil, honey, salt and cracked pepper.
3 Heat 1 tablespoon of butter in a frying pan over medium heat. Use a ladle to scoop up a portion of the batter and pour it into the frying pan. Fry the pancake for 2–4 minutes or until the mixture starts to bubble. Flip over the pancake carefully and fry the other side for 2 minutes.
4 Remove the pancake from the frying pan and place it onto a piece of paper towel to absorb the extra oil. Repeat the process until all of the pancake batter is used.
5 Serve the pancakes with a few lemon wedges, or a poached egg if you're really hungry.

Use

2 cups (300 g/10½ oz) spelt flour
1 teaspoon baking powder
1½ cups (375 ml/13 fl oz) water
1 egg
½ cup (15 g/½ oz) English spinach, finely chopped
½ cup (25 g/1 oz) finely chopped chives
2 teaspoons soy sauce
2 teaspoons sesame oil
1 teaspoon honey
Salt and cracked black pepper, to taste
Butter, for frying
Lemon wedges, to serve

Feel free to replace the English spinach with kale if it's going crazy in the garden.

Seasonal plants and recipes

Chocolate, orange and pistachio salami

Makes 2 salamis

This is not only one of the easiest recipes to create, but it is also the star of the dinner party show for its chewy texture and tangy, full-bodied flavour. It is addictive!

Do

1 In a frying pan over medium heat, lightly toast your slivered almonds until they are golden brown. Roughly chop them and then set them aside.

2 Place the chocolate and butter into a metal bowl over a saucepan of hot water, making sure the base of the bowl isn't touching the water. Keep over low heat until the ingredients are completely melted, stirring to combine. Ensure the chocolate doesn't burn.

3 Place the chocolate mixture into a small bowl. Add the Amaretto and mix well.

4 Once the chocolate mixture has cooled slightly, add the almonds, pistachios, amaretti biscuits and orange zest. Combine everything together well so that all the ingredients are covered in chocolate.

5 Place the mixture into the fridge for 30–45 minutes. Check it after 30 minutes to see how much it has hardened. It should have hardened significantly but still be malleable so you can shape it.

6 Spread a large piece of plastic wrap over your bench. Place half of the chocolate mixture into the centre of the wrap and shape it into a log that is about 5 cm (2 in) in diameter.

7 Tightly cover the salami with the plastic wrap and secure the ends with twine or twist ties. Roll the salami back and forth in the plastic wrap to create a compact, even shape.

8 Repeat the process with the other half of the mixture.

9 Place the salamis into the fridge for at least 6 hours, or ideally overnight.

10 When you are ready to serve the salamis, take them out of the fridge and remove the plastic wrap. Dust a clean surface with icing sugar and roll the salamis until they are coated. Shake off any excess.

11 Using a super-sharp knife, carefully slice the salamis into 1-cm (½-in) thick pieces and serve.

Use

½ cup (65 g/2¼ oz) slivered almonds

50 g (1¾ oz) dark chocolate (we use Lindt, 85% cocoa)

50 g (1¾ oz) milk chocolate (again, Lindt is our preference)

120 g (4¼ oz) salted butter

2 tablespoons Amaretto

1 cup (150 g/5½ oz) pistachios, shelled and roughly chopped

½ cup (60 g/2¼ oz) amaretti biscuits, roughly chopped

1 teaspoon grated orange zest

2 tablespoons icing (confectioners') sugar

Oh and you can replace the orange zest with pitted cherries – yum!

Upside-down blood orange and turmeric cake

Serves 6–8

Cutting into a blood orange is like opening a present. The outside is unassuming, but the inside is boldly beautiful. We decided to make this an upside-down cake to show off the beauty of the blood oranges and not hide them inside the cake. Turmeric is super easy to grow and adds warmth to winter meals, both savoury and sweet.

Do

1 Boil both of the large oranges as per step 1 of the miso, orange and tahini sauce recipe on page 219.

2 Chop the cooled oranges into wedges and remove any pips. Place the oranges and turmeric into a food processor and blend until the mixture is pulpy.

3 Now prepare the blood oranges. In a medium frying pan, bring the water and sugar to a simmer over low heat, stirring until the sugar has dissolved. Add the blood orange slices and vanilla beans. Simmer for 25–35 minutes. Remove the blood orange slices from the frying pan and set them aside to cool.

4 Preheat the oven to 180°C (350°F). Line a 22-cm (8½-in) diameter round cake tin with baking paper.

5 Place the blood orange slices into the base of the cake tin, slightly overlapping each other. Work outwards from the centre.

6 Whisk the eggs and caster sugar together until the mixture is light and fluffy. Add in the orange pulp, almond meal and baking powder. Stir gently until the mixture is combined.

7 Pour the mixture into the cake tin and place it into the oven. Bake the cake for about 1 hour or until the cake is golden and a skewer comes out clean when inserted into the middle.

8 Transfer the cake to a wire rack and allow it to cool in the tin. When the cake has cooled, carefully remove it from the tin and gently peel off the baking paper.

9 Brush the blood orange-covered top with any remaining syrup. Serve the cake with ice-cream or thick Greek-style yoghurt.

Use

For the cake

2 large oranges

1 heaped tablespoon peeled and finely grated fresh turmeric

6 eggs

1 cup (220 g/7¾ oz) caster (superfine) sugar

2 cups (200 g/7 oz) almond meal

1 teaspoon baking powder

For the blood oranges

1 cup (250 ml/9 fl oz) water

2 cups (440 g/15½ oz) caster (superfine) sugar

2–3 blood oranges, thinly sliced on a mandoline

2 vanilla beans

Remember to add some rosemary sprigs to the frying pan to infuse the syrup with an earthier flavour. The rosemary pairs so well with the blood oranges!

Get Growing.

In her book *The Writing Life*, Annie Dillard says, 'How we spend our days is of course how we spend our lives. What we do with this hour and that one is what we are doing.'

The older I get, the more this sentiment rings true. I'm forever reminded that it is our daily habits that define the richness of our lives. It's not the romanticised visions we have of a slower, more fulfilled life when we get this done or complete that task, or the reward we anticipate at the end of our busy journey – but, in fact, what we are doing in this present moment.

Although the demands of modern life will never cease to pull us in all directions, it's important to remember that how we engage with our daily obligations is entirely up to us. For Tess and me, it's a constant struggle to carve out our lives in the direction of joy and happiness, away from work and stress.

We are living in an interesting time, when people's to-do lists are growing exponentially and yet their yearning for and awareness of the good life is also growing. People are waking up to the reality that we are more than our work, and that there is a whole life to be lived. Collectively, we're seeing a shift as people rediscover the joy of growing and cooking. Our urban landscapes – backyards, rooftops, courtyards and balconies – are lighting up with sprouts of herbs, ballooning with fruits and bursting with vegies. Slowly, but I certainly believe surely, people are embracing the joy of gardening and the slower life it brings. There is a change in the air, and we are excited to watch it unfold.

Tess and I are so lucky to have our garden and kitchen as opportunities for slowing down and our daily reminders of the good life. Every seed we have sown and every meal we have cooked has contributed to a better, more fulfilled life for us.

If you're ready to slow down and enjoy the good life, let the garden be your first stop. It doesn't matter the size, or your skill, the garden is a place for everyone. Tuck this book under your arm and grab a beer with the other – the time to slow down and grow is now.

The good life is waiting for you.

Get Growing.

Index.

Thanks.

A big thanks goes to you, for picking up this book and believing in what we do.
Thank you to all the people with whom we've had the pleasure of growing food.
Thanks for sharing your stories, values and what gardening means to you. Your
curiosity, harvests, triumphs (and failures) helped us to define the words and
images needed to bring this book to life.

BYRON

Special thanks to Mum for creating a childhood environment (including magical gardens) that set my core values, which are reflected here in this book.

To Dad for showing us how to live sustainably and planting an orchard we're still picking from today.

To my down-to-earth horticulture teacher, Jeremy Smith, and also to half-plant/half-man Daniel Preston – I've learned too much from you both.

To everyone who has worn a pair of Urban Growers overalls at some point and got into the garden next to me, thank you for making my ideas a reality.

To the Three Blue Ducks team and Grant LaBrooy, thank you for letting us grow food at your restaurants and inspiring this journey.

To the Bondi Public School staff, parents and students! Teaching your garden program was one of the most rewarding and fulfilling chapters of my life. Thanks for having me.

To Campbell Smith for your fine craftsmanship, and Curtis Champion for peer review.

To Sara Wilkinson for sharing your time, knowledge and resources on how to create greener cities.

To Doug and Vicky – your passion for bees has worn off on me, thanks for all your help.

And to Jane, it's a book! Thank you for your guidance in getting this published.

TESS

A special thank you to my parents for giving me every opportunity under the sun and for instilling in me the confidence to make any dream a reality. To Mum for painstakingly reviewing this book with us, and to Dad for inspiring me to get in the kitchen from such a young age.

To my Smack Bang Gang, thank you for giving me the space to create and for supporting me while I tackle a million other projects, like this special one.

To Alex, thank you for your great eye – you've captured the essence of Urban Growers since day one.

To Katie and Jane, thank you for trialling my recipes and being so generous with your time.

To Jane, Jacqui, the whole Murdoch team and its collaborators, thanks for bringing our vision to life with ease.

To Biz and Cam, thanks for your backyard delights, generosity and always damn good company.

And to Byron, thank you for introducing me to this way of life. You make the world a better place.

Published in 2018 by Murdoch Books, an imprint of Allen & Unwin

Murdoch Books Australia
83 Alexander Street
Crows Nest NSW 2065
Phone: +61 (0) 2 8425 0100
murdochbooks.com.au
info@murdochbooks.com.au

Murdoch Books UK
Ormond House
26–27 Boswell Street
London WC1N 3JZ
Phone: +44 (0) 20 8785 5995
murdochbooks.co.uk
info@murdochbooks.co.uk

For Corporate Orders & Custom Publishing, contact our Business Development Team at
salesenquiries@murdochbooks.com.au.

Publisher: Jane Morrow
Editorial Manager: Julie Mazur Tribe
Creative Direction: Dan Peterson and Jacqui Porter, northwoodgreen.com
Project Editor: Dannielle Viera
Photographers: Alex Carlyle (location photography) and Rob Palmer (food photography)
Stylist: Emma Knowles
Home Economists: Ross Dobson and Maxwell Adey
Production Director: Lou Playfair

A cataloguing-in-publication entry is available from the catalogue of the National Library of Australia at nla.gov.au.

ISBN 978 1 76063 176 5 Australia
ISBN 978 1 76063 431 5 UK

A catalogue record for this book is available from the British Library.

Colour reproduction by Splitting Image Colour Studio Pty Ltd, Clayton, Victoria
Printed by Leo Paper Group, China

OVEN GUIDE

You may find cooking times vary depending on the oven you are using. For fan-forced ovens, as a general rule, set the oven temperature to 20°C (70°F) lower than indicated in the recipe.

MEASURES GUIDE

We have used 20 ml (4 teaspoon) tablespoon measures. If you are using a 15 ml (3 teaspoon) tablespoon, add an extra teaspoon of the ingredient for each tablespoon specified.